FIRST STEPS

IN

ANGLO SAXON

FIRST STEPS

IN

ANGLO SAXON

HENRY SWEET

GYAN

Published by

Gyan Publishing House
5, Ansari Road
Daryaganj, New Delhi-110002
Phone: 011-47034999, 9811692060
E-mail: books@gyanbooks.com

Distribution Network
gyanbooks.com
India, USA, Canada, UK, Australia

ISBN: 978-93-7014-648-8 (PB)

First Published, 1897

2nd Impression 2025

Printed at: Gyan Press, Delhi.

FIRST STEPS IN ANGLO SAXON

Author: HENRY SWEET

Clarendon Press Series

FIRST STEPS

IN

ANGLO-SAXON

BY

HENRY SWEET, M.A., PH.D., LL.D.

CORRESPONDING MEMBER
OF THE MUNICH ACADEMY OF SCIENCES

Oxford
AT THE CLARENDON PRESS
1897

PREFACE

In my *Anglo-Saxon Primer* I tried to make things easy for the beginner by adopting a uniform normalized spelling, by giving only a few texts of the simplest character, and by basing the grammar and glossary exclusively on these texts, so that everything learnt in the grammar might be at once utilized in reading the texts, and the time and trouble of looking up words be reduced to a minimum.

But although the *Primer* is perfectly well suited for those students who have already had some linguistic training—especially those who know German—there are others for whom a rigorous grammar-and-glossary method is too abstract, and whose memories will not bear the strain of having to master a grammar of some length before proceeding to the texts.

Such learners require a less concise and abstract exposition, one in which the strain on the memory is reduced to a minimum, partly by careful gradation of difficulties, partly by greater fullness of exposition, and lastly by further simplification and omission of whatever is not absolutely necessary for the learner's first start. The present work shows that these changes do not entail any increase of bulk, the greater fullness of exposition being balanced by the omissions.

As the *Primer* is intended as an introduction to a scientific as well as a purely practical knowledge of Old English, it includes an exposition of some of the fundamental facts of historical grammar, such as the laws of mutation and gradation, which are certainly not necessary for the beginner, even if we admit that they have a practical value in helping to fix the forms in the memory. I have, accordingly, rigorously excluded all such details from the grammar in the present work, which is intended to be a purely practical introduction to the language.

But a practical mastery itself has different stages. The first requisite is to understand written texts, which involves only the power of recognizing grammatical forms, not of constructing them, as in the further stage of writing or speaking the language. Thus in beginning the second text in the present book (§ 14) a learner in the first stage is expected to find out for himself that *manna* is in the genitive plural, and that *cræftum* is in the dative plural, and to infer from the ending *-ne* in *hwelčne* that *cræft* is masculine. He will then be able to infer with tolerable certainty from what he has learnt in the grammar that the plural of *cræft* is *cræftas*, but this inference belongs really to the second stage: a learner in the first stage is expected only to recognize the inflection of *cræftas* when he meets it.

The first object, therefore, of a simplified grammar is to give what is necessary to enable the beginner to recognize the grammatical forms which occur in the texts he is about to read. This excludes not only mutation &c., but also part of the syntax; thus an exposition of the laws of Old English word-order would evidently be out of place in the present grammar.

The first thing is to explain the general structure of the

language—that in Old English, for instance, nouns have three genders, that the gender is partly grammatical, that nouns have four cases—and to state those general rules which admit of no exception, such as that Old English nouns in *-a* are masculine, and that compound nouns follow the gender of their last element.

Those irregular forms which are of very frequent occurrence—such as the inflections of the definite article—must, of course, be learnt by heart at once, the learner relying on their incessant repetition to fix them in his memory. Less frequent irregularities need not be included in the grammar at all, their explanation being relegated to a note. Thus in the present texts the dative *mȩnn* does not occur till near the end (§ 230), where, accordingly, it is explained for the first time. So also with the passive *hātte* (§ 100).

In dealing with a group of irregular forms, we always have to ask ourselves the question, 'Which is the easier for the learner, to bring these forms under general rules, or simply to let them be learnt one by one as they occur?' Experience shows that at first it is better to err in the latter extreme. Accordingly, in dealing with the strong verbs, it will be seen that after giving a general account of their formation, and a few general rules—such as that in the preterite the second person singular always has the same vowel as the plural—I content myself with giving the typical forms of each verb in a note to the passage where it first occurs. When the learner passes on to the *Primer*, he will be able to combine these isolated inflections into a systematic scheme, with most of whose details he will be already familiar.

In some cases where there is more than one form, but without there being any great complexity and irregularity, I steer a middle course: I mention the various forms, but without giving any rules for their use. Thus in § 16 I merely say that 'most strong neuters take *-u* in the plural, or else remain unchanged.' Here the reader will ask 'Why not give the simple rule that *-u* is used only when the preceding syllable is short?' But how about *rīċu*? And if we add a definition of 'short syllable,' and explain all the apparent or real exceptions, our brief rule—which gives all the information required for our purpose—will be considerably lengthened. And if the rest of the grammar is expanded in the same way, it will become simply a reprint of the greater part of the grammar in the *Primer*.

In the grammar I have been careful to group parallel forms together as much as possible. Thus under 'Cases' I give the inflections of nouns, the definite articles, and the personal pronouns all together, so that, for instance, the learner may make *them*, *her* stepping-stones to *þǣm*, *hire*, *þǣre*, and afterwards to the corresponding strong adjective inflections.

The occasional paradigms are in most cases not intended to be learnt by heart, but serve only to sum up the scattered information already given.

All these principles are those which are carried out—consciously or unconsciously—by most linguists. An experienced linguist in attacking a new language begins with the shortest grammar he can find. He first takes a general bird's-eye view of the language, finds out what are its special difficulties, what is to be brought under general rules, what to learn detail by detail, what to put off till a later stage. The rash beginner who starts with a big grammar forgets two-thirds of it soon after he begins independent reading. Such a grammar as the one in the present work simply attempts to give him the really useful residue which, when once learnt, is not and cannot be forgotten.

Inflections may be recognized in two ways: by their form —as when we know that a noun is in the dative plural by its ending in *-um*; or by their function—as when we infer from a word expressing more than one person and standing in the indirect-object relation that it is a noun in the dative plural. Of these two methods of parsing—the formal and the syntactical—sometimes one is easier, sometimes the other. There is, therefore, every reason why elementary syntax should be learnt simultaneously with accidence. It seems irrational to force a beginner to recognize such a grammatical category as the subjunctive mood solely by irregular and perplexing inflections, when such a simple rule as that 'it is always used in indirect narration' may enable him to recognize a large number of subjunctives with mathematical certainty. In my grammar I have therefore blended the two together, which has the further advantage of giving the learner additional examples of the inflections in complete sentences.

The examples in the grammar have been carefully selected so as to prepare the learner for the texts. Those which are not sentences are generally groups of words, so as to do justice to the principle of association. It will be observed that the same principles are followed in the paradigms also. The examples under 'Pronunciation' have been utilized as a preparation for learning the inflections, especially the irregular ones, which offer no more difficulty than the regular ones to the learner who has not yet begun to analyze grammatically.

When an example is repeated, the learner is referred back to it. Thus when he comes to the numerals (§ 56) he finds that nearly all the inflections of *twā* are familiar to him from the examples there repeated.

In accordance with these principles of gradation and comparison, there is no glossary to the texts, but each new word is explained in the notes, or a reference is given to an earlier —rarely a later—explanation. Of course these references are not repeated an indefinite number of times, although I have been careful to err on the safe side, and to make every allowance for defective memories. Often the reference is not to the explanation itself, but to the last passage in which the word occurs, where a reference to the explanation itself will be found. The object of all this is, of course, to give the learner an inducement to master each page of the book thoroughly before proceeding to the next.

I have carried out the same principles with the examples in the grammar: all new words in them after § 22 are explained in the notes, no complete translations being given, so that the learner is obliged to study them with the same care as the texts themselves.

As the limited number of original Old English texts suitable for beginners was nearly exhausted in my *Anglo-Saxon Reader*, I was obliged in the *Primer* to rely mainly on Biblical extracts and Homilies. In the present book I have made new texts by free adaptation of existing texts suitable in matter but not in form. By way of introduction I have taken some passages of Bede's Astronomy, with some alterations and additions. My second text is the gloss to the celebrated *Colloquy of Ælfric*, normalized and put into idiomatic Old English. I have, lastly, paraphrased the first part of *Bēowulf* into simple prose—a translation is, of course, out of the question. In this very difficult task I have been more successful than I expected, although I cannot hope entirely to have escaped errors. These three texts not only form an easy and interesting introduction to the language, but have the further advantage of giving a brief but comprehensive view of the science, daily life, and epic and mythological traditions of our forefathers.

The learner who has worked conscientiously through this little book will have a considerable practical knowledge of the language—a knowledge which will be none the worse for being mainly unconscious and instinctive rather than systematic and analytic. A few weeks' work at the *Primer* will then systematize his knowledge and round it off, and he will proceed to the elements of historical and comparative grammar with all the more zest through not having had them crammed into him prematurely. Some may prefer to use the two books simultaneously. Others who have already gone through the *Primer* will welcome *First Steps* as a means of testing and strengthening their knowledge, and as a relief from the dryness of the texts in the former book.

HENRY SWEET.

MALVERN,
July 22, 1897.

CONTENTS

FIRST STEPS IN ANGLO-SAXON

GRAMMAR

Pronunciation.

1. WHEN the stress (accent) falls on the first syllable of a word of more than one syllable, it is not marked; thus *andswaru* 'answer' has the stress on the same syllable as in Modern English. If the stress falls on any other than the first syllable, it is marked by (·) preceding the letter on which the stress begins; thus *be·sęttan* has the same stress as *besetting*. But we omit the (·) after the prefixes *be-* and *ġe-*, as they never take the stress: *besęttan*, *ġehīeran* (6)= *ġe·hīeran*.

Vowels.

2. The vowels are either short or long. The **short** vowels are left unmarked, the **long** vowels are marked with (¯).

Thus **a** has the sound of the first vowel in *aha!*, and *ā* has the sound of the second: *ān mann* 'one man', *twā handa* 'two hands'.

æ has the sound of the English vowel in *at*, *ǣ* having, of course, the same sound long: *æt hām* 'at home', *mǣre dǣda* 'famous deeds'.

e has the sound of close French *é*: *fela manna* 'many men', *twēgen fēt* 'two feet'.

ę as in *men*: *twēgen męnn* 'two men'.

i close, as in French *fini*: *fīf fingras* 'five fingers'.

ie has the open sound of *i* in *it*: *hīe wǣron iernende* 'they were running'.

o close, as in French *beau*: *Godes word* 'God's word', *gōd wīn* 'good wine'.

u close, as in French *sou*: *mīn sunu* 'my son'; *twā hūs* 'two houses'.

y as in French *lu*: *se cyning* 'the king', *lȳtel hūs* 'a little house'. (Observe that the indefinite article is generally omitted.)

3. There are also diphthongs, which have the stress on the first element:—

ea=*ǽa* (*æ* in *æt* followed by the *a* in *mann*): *heard stān* 'a hard stone', *hēah weall* 'a high wall'.

eo is pronounced as written, with two close vowels: *fēower sweord* 'four swords'.

Consonants.

4. Double consonants must be pronounced really double or long. Thus, whilst *n* in *sunu* (2) is pronounced as in *money*, the *nn* in *sēo sunne* 'the sun' is pronounced as in *pen-knife*.

5. c has the sound of *k*: *cēne cęmpa* 'a brave warrior', *lȳtel cnapa* 'a little boy'.

ċ is a *k* formed in that part of the mouth where we form the *y* in *you*: *sēo ċiriċe* 'the church', *styċċemǣlum* 'piecemeal, bit by bit'.

6. g at the beginning of words and in the combination *ng* is pronounced as in *go*: *þæt grēne gærs* 'the green grass', *þæt langsċip* 'the war-ship (long ship)'. Otherwise, that is after vowels and *l*, *r*, it has the sound of German *g* in *sagen*: *twēġen dagas* 'two days', *miċel burg* 'a great city', *se hālga* 'the saint (the holy one)'.

ġ in the combination *nġ* has a sound analogous to that of *ċ*, something like the *g* in *gem*: *mẹnġan* 'mingle, mix'. Also in *cg*, which is pronounced as if written *ġġ*: *wǣpnes ẹcg* 'the edge of a weapon'. Also at the beginning of words and syllables, as in *ġeond middanġeard* 'throughout the world', except that in unaccented syllables it had the sound of our *y*, as in *ġehīeran* 'to hear'. Otherwise, that is after all vowels and all consonants except *n*, it had the sound of our *y* in *you*: *hāliġe ẹnġlas* 'holy angels', *ā·wierġed sċucca* 'an accursed sprite (demon)'.

7. h at the beginning of a syllable has the same sound as now: *hē hæfþ hund* 'he has a dog'. Otherwise it has the sound of German *ch*: *nēah* 'near', *sēo sulh* 'the plough', *beorht* 'bright'. *hw*, as in *hwæt* 'what', has the sound of our *wh*. *hl, hn, hr* differ from *l, n, r* respectively in the same way as *hw* differ from *w*, *hl* having the sound of Welsh *ll*: *se hlāford* 'the lord', *hnītan* 'to collide', *hrædliċe* 'quickly'.

8. þ may be pronounced as the 'breath' *th* in *thin* at the beginning and end of words, and after breath consonants such as *c*, *p*: *sōþ þū sẹġst* 'you speak the truth', *hē slǣpþ* 'he sleeps'. Otherwise, that is when followed by a vowel and preceded by a vowel or a 'voice' consonant such as *r*, it had the voice sound in *then*: *on heofone and on eorþan* 'in heaven and on earth'.

9. f and **s** have the breath sounds *f*, *s* and the voice sounds *v*, *z* according to the same rules. Thus they have the breath sound in *se fēond* 'the enemy', *se hlāf* 'the loaf, the bread', *swā wīs* 'so wise', and when doubled, as in *lǣssa* 'less';

the voice sound in *heofon* 'heaven', *se wīsa lārēow* 'the wise teacher', *hē rǣsde on hine* 'he rushed on him'.

10. **r** and **w** must be pronounced clearly wherever they are written: *hēr* 'here', *þæt word* 'the word', *se wrećća* 'the exile', *þæt trēow* 'the tree'.

Nouns.

Gender.

11. Every noun has one of three genders, which are most easily remembered by learning each noun with the definite article 'the'—masculine *se*, neuter *þæt*, feminine *sēo*. The gender is partly natural, partly grammatical. By the natural gender names of male beings, such as *se fæder* 'the father', *se brōþor* 'the brother', are masculine; those of female beings, such as *seō mōdor* 'the mother', *sēo dohtor* 'the daughter', are feminine; and those of young creatures, such as *þæt ćild* 'the child', are neuter. But *þæt wīf* 'the woman, wife' is also neuter.

12. By grammatical gender names of things are not only neuter—*þæt hūs* 'the house', *þæt ēage* 'the eye'—but also masculine and feminine: *se stān* (3), *se fōt* 'the foot'; *sēo hand* (2), *sēo dǣd* (2). Note that all nouns ending in *-a* are masculine: *se lȳtla cnapa* (5), *se nama* 'the name', *se mōna* 'the moon'.

13. Compound nouns follow the gender of their last element, as in *se goldsmiþ* 'the goldsmith', formed from *þæt gold* 'the gold' and *se smiþ* 'the smith', *se wīfmann* 'woman' from *þæt wīf* (11) and *se mann* (2).

Number.

14. The definite article has in the plural *þā* for all genders. Nouns have a variety of endings in the plural, which depend partly on their gender. Nouns in *-a*—which are all masculine (12)—take *-an* in the plural: *þā naman* (12), *þā lȳtlan cnapan*. All feminine nouns in *-e*, together with *þæt ēage* (12), have the same plural ending: *twā* (2) *ċiriċan* (5), *twā ēagan*.

Nouns that take *-an* in the plural are called **weak**. All other nouns are called **strong**.

15. The commonest plural-ending of strong masculine nouns is *-as*; thus *se cyning* (2), *se ęnde* 'end' have plurals *cyningas*, *ęndas*. *se dæġ* has plural *dagas* (6) with vowel-change.

16. Most strong neuters take *-u* in the plural, or else remain unchanged; thus *þæt sċip* 'ship', *þæt rīċe* 'kingdom, rule, sovereignty', *þæt wǣpen* 'weapon' (6) have plurals *þā sċipu*, *þā rīċu*, *þā wǣpnu*, while *þæt folc* 'nation', *þæt hūs* (2), *þæt wīf* (11) have plurals *þā folc*, *þā hūs*, *þā wīf*.

17. Most strong feminines take *-a* in the plural; thus *sēo dǣd* (2), *sēo hand* (2), *sēo ċeaster* 'city' have plurals *þā dǣda*, *þā handa*, *þā ċeastra*.

18. Some plurals are formed by vowel-change: *se mann*, *þā męnn* (2); *se fōt* (12), *þā fēt* (2); *sēo bōc* 'the book', *þā bēċ*; *sēo burg* 'fortress, city', *þā byriġ*. There are also other irregular plurals.

Case.

19. All the nouns hitherto given in this chapter are in the **nominative** case. We have seen that weak masculine nouns have in the nominative singular the ending *-a* (*se mōna*), weak feminines and neuters the ending *-e* (*sēo ċiriċe*, *þæt ēage*). Nouns ending in *-u* and *-o* are always strong, such as *se sunu* (2), *sēo duru* 'door', plurals *þā suna*, *þā dura*, *sēo ieldo* 'age, old age' (*eald* 'old'), *sēo męniġo* 'multitude, crowd' (*manig* 'many'). Note that these feminines in *-o* are generally indeclinable, as in the plural *þā męnigo*.

The following are pronouns in the nominative: *iċ* 'I', *þū* (8); *hē* (7), *hit* 'it', *hēo* 'she', plurals *wē* 'we', *ġē* 'ye', *hīe* (2). Further examples: *iċ eom hēr* 'I am here' | *hēo is mīn* (2) *mōdor* (11) | *hit is lȳtel* (2) *hūs* (16) | *ġē wīf!* (16).

20. The subject of a sentence and words agreeing with it are put in the nominative: *iċ eom þæs cyninges hunta* 'I am the king's hunter'.

Nouns have three other cases, the accusative, dative, and genitive, included under the common name 'oblique'.

21. The **accusative** of the definite article is masculine *þone*, feminine *þā*, the neuter *þæt* and the plural (all genders) *þā* being the same as the nominative. Note that in all words the accusative is the same as the nominative in the neuter singular (*þæt ēage*), and in the plural (*þā cyningas*).

22. The accusative is the direct-object case, serving to show that a noun-word completes the meaning of a transitive verb.

23. Weak masculine and feminine nouns have accusative singulars in *-an* (the same as the plural nominative): *iċ ġehīerde þone naman* (12) | *wē ġesāwon þā sunnan* (4) *and þone mōnan* (12).

24. Strong masculine (as well as neuter) nouns have the accusative the same as the nominative in the singular as well as the plural: *hē grētte þone cyning*.

25. Some strong feminines have the accusative singular the same as the nominative, while others take *-e*: *iċ ġeseah þā undǣd* | *hīe ġesāwon* (23) *þā ċeastre* (17) *feorran*.

26. The accusatives of the pronouns given above (19) are *mē* 'me', *þē* 'thee', *hine* (9) 'him', *hit* (the same as the nom.,

21) 'it', *hīe* 'her', plurals *ūs* 'us', *eow* 'you', *hīe* 'them'. Observe that the Modern English forms *him*, *her*, *them* are historically datives (29) not accusatives. Compare further *hine* with *þone* (21), *hī-e* 'her' with *þā ċeastr-e*. The following are further examples: *canst þū þisne cræft? iċ cann hine* | *ġesihst þū þā ċeastre? iċ hīe ġesēo.*

. **27.** The accusative is further used to express extent of space and duration of time: *iċ eom* (20) *ealneweġ ġearo* | *hīe wunodon þǣr lange tīd.*

28. Hence some prepositions which express extent or motion govern the accusative, such as *ġeond* (6) 'throughout', *ymb* 'around, about': *ġeond þā healle* | *sēo sunne* (23) *iernþ ymb þā eorþan.*

29. The **dative** of *se*, *þæt* and the plural *þā* is *þǣm*. Similarly the dative of *hē*, *hit* and the plural *hīe* is *him* 'him, it, them' (compare Modern English *to hi-m, to the-m*). Note also that the dative plural ending of nearly all nouns is *-um*. The dative of *sēo* is *þǣre*. Similarly the dative of *hēo* is *hire* (compare Modern English *to he-r*). The pronouns *iċ*, *þū*, plurals *wē*, *ġē*, have the dative the same as the accusative: *mē* 'to me', *þē* 'to thee', *ūs* 'to us', *ēow* 'to you'.

30. The dative is the indirect-object case; and often corresponds to the Modern English 'to' in 'give it to him', 'similar to': *sęle mē hafoc! hwæt sċeal iċ þīnum ġebrōþrum sęllan? sęle him hors!*

31. Weak nouns have dative singular in *-an*: *God sealde þǣm mōnan* (12) *leoht.*

32. Most strong nouns have *-e* in the dative singular: *slǣp biþ dēaþe ġelīcost* | *hē andswarode hire þus. sēo andswaru ġelīcode þǣre cwēne* | *hīe sind þǣm cyninge ġetrīewe.*

33. The dative is used not only with verbs of giving to, speaking to, and with words expressing nearness to, likeness to, being agreeable to, faithful to, and so on, but also with many other words expressing benefiting and injuring, affecting and influencing in various ways: *eallum mannum nytt* | *hē him on-bestæl* | *hē ċearf him þæt hēafod of* | *fisċeras bregdaþ him nętt.*

For the 'instrumental dative' see 52.

34. Many prepositions govern the dative, such as *æfter* 'after', *be* 'by, along, concerning', *for* 'for, because of', *mid* 'with', *tō* 'to': *æfter his dæġe* | *hē ēode be þǣre strǣte* | *wacian for þēofum* | *se cyning sæt mid his ealdormannum* | *hē cwæþ tō þǣm cyninge.*

35. Some prepositions govern both the dative and accusative, such as *on* 'in, on' (8, 9), *ofer* 'over', *under* 'under'. When motion or extension is implied they generally take the accusative (28): *se mangere āstāg on his sċip* | *þā bēamas hangiaþ ofer þone męre.* With the dative they generally express rest: *se fisċere* (33) *is ūte on þǣre sǣ* (46) *on ānum bāte.*

36. The **genitive** corresponds sometimes to *'s* (*man's*), sometimes to *of* (*of the man*).

37. The genitive of *se* and *þæt* is *þæs* (20). Similarly the genitive of *hē* and *hit* 'it' is *his*. The genitive of *sēo* is *þǣre* —the same as the dative. Similarly the genitive of *hēo* 'she' is *hire*. The genitive of the plural *þā* is *þāra*. Similarly the genitive of *hīe* 'they' is *hira*. The pronouns *iċ*, *þū*, plural *wē*, *ġē*, have genitives *mīn* 'of me', *þīn* 'of thee', *ūre* 'of us', *ēower* 'of you'. The genitives of pronouns are used also as possessives: *hīe sind* (32) *hira hlāforde* (7) *getrīewe* (32). The following are examples of their use as genitives: *ēower nān* | *hē ofslōg hira þrītiġ.*

38. Weak nouns have genitive singular *-an*—the same as

the other oblique cases—and genitive plural *-ena*: *þæs mōnan leoht* (31) *and þāra steorrena* | *þǣre sunnan* (23) *hǣte*.

39. Strong masculine and neuter nouns have genitive singular in *-es*, plural in *-a*: *þæs cyninges heall* (28) | *þæt hūs is ealra* (33) *hūsa bętst*.

40. Strong feminines have genitive singular *-e*—the same as the dative—and generally genitive plural *-a*: *þǣre healle duru* | *ealra* (39) *dǣda* (17) *mǣrost*.

41. The genitive is used instead of the accusative with verbs expressing thinking of, being mindful of, remembering, and other mental states, and various emotions: *hē ġemundę þāra worda þe hē ǣr spræc* | *yfeles wēnan* | *hīe fæġnodon þæs ġebēorsċipes*.

42. Also with some verbs of having possession or enjoyment of, striving for: *sweordes onfōn* | *mętes brūcan* | *þā fiend his ehton*.

43. Some of these verbs govern a genitive of the thing and an accusative of the person, especially those which express asking: *hīe hine friþes bǣdon*.

44. Some of them have a dative of the person, especially those expressing granting or denying: *hē him friþes ġetīþode* | *hē þancode hire þæs*.

45. The following table will show the chief noun-inflections:—

Sing.	Nom.	*se dæġ*	*þæt hūs, sċip*	*sēo ċeaster, dǣd*
	Acc.	*þone dæġ*	*þæt hūs*	*þā ċeastre, dǣd*
	Dat.	*þǣm dæġe*	*þǣm hūse*	*þǣre ċeastre*
	Gen.	*þæs dæġes*	*þæs hūses*	*þǣre ċeastre*
Plur.	Nom.	*þā dagas*	*þā hūs, sċipu*	*þā ċeastra*
	Dat.	*þǣm dagum*	*þǣm hūsum*	*þǣm ċeastrum*
	Gen.	*þāra daga*	*þāra hūsa*	*þāra ċeastra*

Sing.	Nom.	*se wita*	*þæt ēage*	*sēo ċiriċe*
	Acc.	*þone witan*	*þæt ēage*	*þā ċiriċan*
	Dat.	*þǣm witan*	*þǣm ēagan*	*þǣre ċiriċan*
	Gen.	*þæs witan*	*þæs ēagan*	*þǣre ċiriċan*
Plur.	Nom.	*þā witan*	*þā ēagan*	*þā ċiriċan*
	Dat.	*þǣm witum*	*þǣm ēagum*	*þǣm ċiriċum*
	Gen.	*þāra witena*	*þāra ēagena*	*þāra ċiriċena*

46. Nouns ending in a long vowel or diphthong contract their inflections. Thus *sēo sǣ* (35) has *sǣ* in the oblique cases of the singular: *þǣre sǣ strand.* So also *sēo ēa* 'river' has dative plural *ēam.* The weak noun *ġefēa* 'joy' has *ġefēan* in the oblique singular cases: *mid* (34) *ġefēan.*

47. The body of the word undergoes various changes in inflection. Thus *se feorh* 'life' has genitive *fēores.* In such a word as *þæt feoh* 'money' these changes necessarily result in contraction of the inflection (46): genitive *þæs fēos*, dative *þǣm fēo*: *hē mē þæs fēos ġetiþode* (44).

Adjectives.

48. Adjectives have two kinds of inflection, strong and weak.

The **weak** inflections of adjectives are the same as those of weak nouns, except in the genitive plural, which has the strong adjective form.

Adjectives take weak inflections when preceded by the definite article or other defining words such as 'this':—

	Sing.		
Nom.	*se gōda wita*	*þæt gōde wīf*	*sēo gōde dǣd*
Acc.	*þone gōdan witan*	*þæt gōde wīf*	*þā gōdan dǣd*
Dat.	*þǣm gōdan witan*	*þǣm gōdan wīfe*	*þǣre gōdan dǣde*
Gen.	*þæs gōdan witan*	*bæs gōdan wīfes*	*þǣre gōdan dǣde*

Plur.

Nom.	*þā gōdan witan*	*þā gōdan wīf*	*þā gōdan dǣda*
Dat.	*þǣm gōdum witum*	*þǣm gōdum wīfum*	*þǣm gōdum dǣdum*
Gen.	*þāra gōdra witena*	*þāra gōdra wīfa*	*þāra gōdra dǣda*

49. Otherwise adjectives have **strong** inflections, resembling partly those of strong nouns, but more generally those of the personal pronouns :—

Sing.	Nom.	*gōd cræft*	*gōd ċild*	*gōd cwēn*
	Acc.	*gōdne cræft*	*gōd ċild*	*gōde cwēne*
	Dat.	*gōdum cræfte*	*gōdum ċilde*	*gōdre cwēne*
	Gen.	*gōdes cræftes*	*gōdes ċildes*	*gōdre cwēne*
Plur.	Nom.	*gōde cræftas*	*gōd ċild*	*gōde cwēna*
	Dat.	*gōdum cræftum*	*gōdum ċildum*	*gōdum cwēnum*
	Gen.	*gōdra cræfta*	*gōdra ċilda*	*gōdra cwēna*

50. Some take *-u* in the feminine singular nominative and neuter plural :—

Sing.	Nom.	*sum cræft*	*sum ċild*	*sumu cwēn*
	Acc.	*sumne cræft*	*sum ċild*	*sume cwēne*
Plur.	Nom.	*sume cræftas*	*sumu ċild*	*sume cwēna*

51. The following are examples of the strong inflections of adjectives: *geond* (28) *ealne* (33) *middangeard* | *hē hæfþ* (7) *miċel* (6) *mōd* | *hē wunode þǣr lange tīd* | *gōdum* (2) *cyninge ġedafenaþ þæt hē sīe cystiġ* | *on ānre dīeġelre stōwe* | *mē is gōdes wǣpnes* (16) *þearf* | *þrēo pund gōdre buteran* | *se hunta* (20) *hæfþ swifte hundas* | *eall þā sċipu wǣron nīwu* | *eallum mannum cūþ* | *ealra witena gemōt.*

52. Strong adjectives have an **instrumental** case, but only in the masculine and neuter singular; it has the same form as the dative of nouns, that is *-e*. In the feminine and plural the dative—instrumental dative—is used instead, the dative *-um* being used instrumentally instead of *-e* in the masculine and neuter singular also. The instrumental and instrumental dative are used to express the instrument and manner of an action, and time when: *sprec mildum wordum!* | *þā munucas gāþ tō* (34) *ċiriċan ǣlċe dæġe*. The instrumental is often used with the preposition *mid* (34): *mid miċle* (51) *nīþe*.

Comparison.

53. The **comparative** is formed by adding *-ra*, and always has weak inflection. Thus from *lēof* 'dear, beloved, pleasant' is formed the comparative masculine *lēofra* 'more dear', neuter and feminine *lēofre*, plural *lēofran*: *þæt* (44) *is mē lēofre*.

54. The **superlative** is formed by adding *-ost*, and is inflected strong or weak in the same way as the positive: *hē is mē ealra manna lēofost* | *se lēofosta mann*.

55. Some adjectives have vowel-change in comparison, in which case the superlative ends in *-est*, as in *eald* 'old', *ieldra, ieldest* | *lang* (27), *lęngra, lęngest*.

Numerals.

56. The first two are inflected thus:—

	MASC.	NEUT.	FEM.	MASC.	NEUT.	FEM.
Nom.	*twēġen*	*twā*	*twā*	*þrīe*	*þrēo*	*þrēo*
Dat.		*twǣm*			*þrim*	
Gen.		*twēġra*			*þrēora*	

Examples: *twēġen męnn* (2), *twā hūs* (2), *twā handa* (2), *mid twǣm handum* | *þrīe męnn, þrēo pund* (51), *þrēora suna* (19) *fæder* (11).

57. The others up to twenty are not inflected. The ty-numerals are sometimes uninflected, sometimes inflected like adjectives: *þrītiġra* (37) *manna mæġen.* When uninflected, the ty-numerals are regarded as nouns, and govern the genitive, not only in a partitive sense, as in *hē ofslōg hira þrītiġ*, but in other constructions: *se cyning hēold þæt rīċe* (16) *fīftiġ wintra.* *þæt hund* 'hundred' and *þæt þūsend* 'thousand' are nouns: *þūsend cēnra cęmpena.*

Pronouns.

58. The following are the inflections of the **personal** pronouns:—

Sing. Nom.	*iċ* 'I'	*þū* 'thou'
Acc.	*mē*	*þē*
Dat.	*mē*	*þē*
Gen.	*mīn*	*þīn*
Dual. Nom.	*wit* 'we two'	*ġit* 'ye two'
Acc.	*unc*	*inc*
Dat.	*unc*	*inc*
Gen.	*uncer*	*incer*
Plur. Nom.	*wē* 'we (three)'	*ġē* 'ye (three)'
Acc.	*ūs*	*ēow*
Dat.	*ūs*	*ēow*
Gen.	*ūre*	*ēower*

Examples of the dual: *se lārēow cwæþ* (34) *tō þǣm twǣm ġebrōþrum* (30) '*hwæt wille ġit þæt iċ inc* (dat.) *dō?*' *þā twēġen ġebrōþru andswarodon* (32) '*wit willaþ þæt þū unc lǣre.*'

59. In addition to the pronouns of the third person, the definite article is used also in the sense of 'this one, he, she' etc., *se* becoming *sē*:—

Sing.	Nom.	*hē, sē*	*hit, þæt*	*hēo, sēo*
	Acc.	*hine, þone*	*hit, þæt*	*hīe, þā*
	Dat.	*him, þǣm*	*him, þǣm*	*hire, þǣre*
	Gen.	*his, þæs*	*his, þæs*	*hire, þǣre*
Plur.	Nom.		*hīe, þā*	
	Dat.		*him, þǣm*	
	Gen.		*hira, þāra*	

Examples of *sē*: *ān* (35) *cyning wæs on* (35) *Dęnum, sē wæs hāten Hrōþgar* | *iċ āsċode hine be þǣm.* The *sē* in the first example may be translated 'who'.

60. The possessive pronouns *mīn* (2), *þīn* (30), *uncer, incer, ūre, ēower*, which are the genitives of the personal pronouns, are inflected as strong adjectives: *mid mīnum handum* | *wē sind ūrum hlāforde getrīewe* (37) | *on ēowerre ċeastre.* The genitives of the third person, *his, hire, hira*, are used as indeclinable possessives, as in *hīe sind on hira āgnum hūse* compared with *wē sind on ūrum āgnum hūse.*

61. The interrogative pronoun *hwā* 'who' has inflections similar to those of *se*:—

	MASC.	NEUT.	FEM.
Nom.	*hwā*	*hwæt*	*hwā*
Acc.	*hwone*	*hwæt*	*hwone*
Dat.		*hwǣm*	
Gen.		*hwæs*	

62. The **demonstrative** *þes* 'this' also has inflections resembling those of *se*:—

		MASC.	NEUT.	FEM.
Sing.	Nom.	*þes*	*þis*	*þēos*
	Acc.	*þisne*	*þis*	*þās*
	Dat.	*þissum*	*þissum*	*þisse*
	Gen.	*þisses*	*þisses*	*þisse*
Plur.	Nom.		*þās*	
	Dat.		*þissum*	
	Gen.		*þissa*	

Examples: *þes ealda* (55, 48) *mann* | *hwanon cōmon ġē hider on þis land?* | *þēos eorþe is swīþe brād* | *sēo sunne iernþ* (28) *ymb þās eorþan* | *on niht sēo sunne is under* (35) *þisse eorþan* | *eall þās þing.*

63. The **relative** pronoun is the indeclinable *þe: þā þing þe iċ dyde.* It is often combined with *sē* to form the inflected relative *sē-þe: hū mæġ sē* (59) *bēon ġesǣliġ sē-þe on þǣm ġesǣlþum þurh·wunian ne mōt?*

Verbs.

64. The **infinitive** of verbs ends in *-an*, which, like other inflections (46), is shortened to *-n* after a vowel, as in *gān* 'to go' compared with *cuman* 'to come': *iċ ġeseah* (25) *þā sċipu tō lanđe* (62) *cuman* | *hwider wilt þū gān?*

65. From the infinitive is formed the **supine** *tō cumanne, tō gānne*, in which the infinitive is put into the dative after the preposition *tō* (34). It is used to express necessity and purpose, and to define: *þā þing þe* (63) *tō dōnne* (58) *sind* (60) | *hīe cōmon þæt land tō sċēaw·ianne* | *fæġer on tō lōcianne.*

66. The **present participle** ends in *-ende, -nde*, as in *iernende* (2), *dōnde* 'doing': *on horsum* (30) *rīdende.* When present participles are made into nouns, they drop the final *e*, as in *se fēond* (42) 'enemy', literally 'hating'.

67. The **preterite participle** generally takes the prefix *ge-*, unless the verb already has some such prefix. It is formed in two ways. In 'strong' verbs it ends in *-en, -n.* Thus the strong verbs *cuman, becuman* 'come', *gān* have preterite participles *cumen, becumen, ġegān* (compare Modern English *go, go-ne*). In 'weak' verbs it ends in *-d, -t.* Thus the weak verb *ġehīeran* (23) has preterite participle *ġehīered.*

68. The finite verb has three moods, indicative, subjunctive, and imperative—of which we are at present concerned only with the first,—and two tenses, present and preterite, together with two numbers, singular and plural, and three persons.

69. In the present (indicative) the first person ends in -(*e*): *iċ cume, iċ ġehīere, iċ gā*; the second in *-st: þū ġehīerst* 'thou hearest'; and the third in *-þ*: *hē ġehīerþ* 'he heareth'. The plural ends in -(*a*)*þ*: *wē ġehīeraþ, ġē cumaþ, hīe gāþ.*

70. The *þ* of the third singular is changed to *t* or lost after some consonants, as in *hē forġiet-t*, from *forġietan* 'forget'. After some consonants it modifies the preceding consonant, and is sometimes dropped itself, as in *hē węnt* from *węndan* 'turn, go', *hē fēt* from *fēdan* 'feed', *hē sęt* from *sęttan* 'set'. The *-st* of the second person often causes similar changes in preceding consonants, as in *þū fētst* 'thou feedest'.

71. Double consonants are always simplified before *-st* and *-þ*, *cg* (=*gg* 6) being made into *ġ*, as in *hē ġefylþ* from *ġefyllan* 'fill', *þū sęġst* from *sęcgan* 'say'.

72. In the preterite the first and third person are always the same—*iċ ġehīerde, hē ġehīerde*—and the plural ends in *-on* in all three persons: *wē ġehīerdon, hīe ġehīerdon.*

Strong Verbs.

73. Strong verbs in addition to the above-described consonant-changes often modify their vowels before *-st* and *-þ*, as in *hwæt itst þū?* *hē itt* from *etan* 'eat', *hē cymþ* from *cuman*, *hē gǣþ* from *gān*.

74. The preterite of strong verbs is formed, not by adding anything, but by various vowel-changes: *iċ cume* 'I come', *iċ cōm* 'I came'; *iċ binde* 'I bind', *iċ band* 'I bound'; *iċ cweþe* (34), *iċ cwæþ*; *iċ ā·rīse* 'I arise', *iċ ā·rās* 'I arose'; *iċ bebēode* 'I command', *iċ bebēad*.

75. The preterite plural sometimes has the same vowel as the singular: *hē cōm*, *hīe cōmon*; *hē hēold*, *hīe hēoldon* from *healdan* (57). But generally the plural has a different vowel: *hē band*, *hīe bundon*; *hē ā·rās*, *hīe ā·rison*; *hē bebēad*, *hīe bebudon*. Sometimes there is consonant-change as well: *hē cwæþ*, *hīe cwǣdon*; *hē hrēas*, *hīe hruron* from *hrēosan* 'fall'.

76. The second person singular of the preterite always has the same vowel and consonant as the preterite plural, from which it can be formed by changing *-on* into *-e*: *hē wæs* 'he was', *hīe wǣron* 'they were', *þū wǣre* 'thou wer-t'. So also *hē spræc*, *þū sprǣce*, *hīe sprǣcon* from *sprecan* (41).

77. The following are the inflections of the very frequent strong verb *weorþan* 'become', including the subjunctive (85):—

		INDICATIVE.	SUBJUNCTIVE.
Pres. Sing.	1.	*iċ weorþe*	*þæt iċ weorþe*
	2.	*þū wierst*	*þæt þū weorþe*
	3.	*hē wierþ*	*þæt hē weorþe*
Plur.		*hīe weorþaþ*	*þæt hīe weorþen*

	INDICATIVE.	SUBJUNCTIVE.
Pret. Sing. 1.	*iċ wearþ*	*þæt iċ wurde*
2.	*þū wurde*	*þæt þū wurde*
3.	*hē wearþ*	*þæt hē wurde*
Plur.	*hīe wurdon*	*þæt hīe wurden*

The preterite participle is *ġeworden*.

Weak Verbs.

78. In weak verbs the second person singular of the preterite is formed by adding *-st*, as in *ġehīerdest þū?*

79. Some weak verbs have infinitive *-an*, some *-ian*. The latter are inflected in two different ways:—

Pres. Sing. 1.	*iċ fęriġe* 'carry'	*iċ wuniġe* 'dwell'
2.	*þū fęrest*	*þū wunast*
3.	*hē fęreþ*	*hē wunaþ*
Plur.	*hīe fęriäþ*	*hīe wuniaþ*
Pret. Sing. 1.	*iċ fęrede*	*iċ wunode*
2.	*þū fęredest*	*þū wunodest*
3.	*hē fęrede*	*hē wunode*
Plur.	*hīe fęredon*	*hīe wunodon*
Partic. Pres.	*fęriende*	*wuniende*
Pret.	*ġefęred*	*ġewunod*
Infin.	*fęrian*	*wunian*
Gerund.	*tō fęrianne*	*tō wunianne*

80. Those with infinitive *-an* are inflected thus:—

	PRESENT.	PRETERITE.
Sing. 1.	*iċ ġehīere*	*iċ ġehīerde*
2.	*þū ġehīerst*	*þū ġehīerdest*
3.	*hē ġehīerþ*	*hē ġehīerde*
Plur.	*hīe ġehīeraþ*	*hīe ġehīerdon*
Partic.	*ġehīerende*	*ġehīered*

81. Some weak verbs omit the *e* in the preterite participle, as in *ġelǣdd* from *lǣdan* 'lead, bring, carry', the *d* itself being lost in such participles as *ā·sęnd* (67) from *ā·sęndan* 'send'.

82. After some consonants the *-de* of the preterite is changed to *-te*, generally with loss or change of the preceding consonant, as in *sętte* from *sęttan* 'set', *tǣhte* from *tǣċan* 'show'. The preterite participle has the same changes: *ġesętt*, *ġetǣht*.

83. Some of these verbs have vowel-change in the preterite and preterite participle, as in *sæġde* from *sęcgan* (71), *sealde* from *sęllan* (30, 31), *worhte* from *wyrcan* 'work, make, do', *sohte* from *sēċan* 'seek', *þohte* from *þęnċan* 'think', preterite participles *ġesæġd*, *ġeseald*, *ġeworht*, *ġesoht*, *ġeþoht*.

Preterite-Present Verbs.

84. These have for their presents old strong preterites, from which new weak preterites are formed, generally with considerable irregularities. Thus *wāt* 'I know, he knows' has plural *wē witon* like *ā·rās*, *ā·rison* (75), preterite *wiste*, plural *wiston*, the infinitive being *witan*. The second person singular present generally ends in *-t* or *-st*: *þū wāst*, *þū canst* 'thou knowest' from *cann* 'knows', plural *hīe cunnon*, preterite *hē cūþe*. Most of them have no infinitive, and they are often otherwise defective.

Subjunctive.

85. The subjunctive mood (compare 77) makes no distinction of persons. In the present singular it has the ending of the first person of the indicative, which is of course dropped after a vowel: *þæt iċ cume* 'that I may come', *þæt þū gā* (indic. *þū gǣst* 73), *þæt hē ġehīere*. The plural ending in the present is *-(e)n*: *þæt wē cumen*, *þæt wē gān*.

The subjunctive present of the verb 'be' is *sīe* (51), plural *sīen*.

86. The preterite subjunctive is formed from the preterite indicative in the same way: *þæt iċ ġehīerde, þæt þū ġehīerde* (indic. *ġehīerdest*), *þæt hē ġehīerde, þæt wē ġehīerden.* In strong verbs the preterite subjunctive has the form of the second person of the indicative: *þæt iċ wǣre, þæt þū wǣre, þæt hē wǣre*; plural *þæt wē wǣren.* So also *bindan* (74) has subjunctive preterite *bunde*, plural *bunden.* In the preterite-present verbs the subjunctive present has the form of a strong subjunctive preterite: *þæt iċ wite, þæt wē witen, þæt hē cunne.*

87. The subjunctive states something not as a fact, but merely as something thought of.

88. In independent sentences it expresses what is wished or commanded: *ġehealde ēow se ælmihtiga!*

Otherwise it is used chiefly in dependent sentences.

89. Thus it is used in indirect narration to show that the speaker is stating something merely as an idea suggested to him by some one else: *hīe cwǣdon* (75) *þæt hē wǣre gōd cyning.* If the truth of the statement is so self-evident that it could be expressed by direct narration without any change of meaning, then the indicative may be used, as in *nū wē willaþ* (58) *seċgan* (83) *þæt wē fūse sind* (65) *ūrne eard tō sēċanne*, which means exactly the same as *nū wē sind fūse . . .*, so that the subjunctive would here be too emphatic: *þæt wē fūse sīen* would imply that the speakers wished to say that their statement was false.

90. So also in indirect question and similar constructions: *hē āsċode* (59) *hwæt hīe wǣren* | *hīe ne mihton ā·þenċan hū* (63) *hīe hira fēondum* (66) *wiþ·standan mihten.*

91. In the following examples the subjunctive evidently expresses something as an idea, not as an accomplished fact:

hē bæd hine þæt hē him tō fultume cōme | *þā męnn belifon þǣr* (27) *bæftan þæt hīe þæt sċip hēolden* (88) | *cyninge ġedafenaþ þæt hē sīe cystiġ* (51) | *hē ūþe him* (them) *þæt hīe mōsten inn cuman* | *miċel pleoh biþ* (32) *þæt man hwæl ġefō*. In *swā hwelċ swā þū sīe, begā þīnne cræft* (26)*!* the subjunctive gives the meaning of indefiniteness, implying 'I do not know who you are'.

92. In some cases the subjunctive implies that the statement is not merely hypothetical, but unreal or impossible, as in hypothetical comparison; thus *hē rīċsode swelċe hē cyning wǣre* implies *hē næs nā cyning*.

93. So also in clauses of rejected condition, where the unreality is further shown by putting the verb in the preterite, as in *ġif þū swā unforht wǣre swā þū self sęġst*, which implies *neart þū swā unforht swā þū self sęġst*.

94. Hence the indicative is often used in clauses of 'open condition', to show that the condition is not rejected, although we should otherwise expect the subjunctive: *iċ þē sęlle hafoc, ġif þū mē sęlst hund* (30).

95. There is a tendency to use the subjunctive in clauses dependent on a negative sentence, as in *neom iċ swā spēdiġ þæt iċ mæġe* (90) *mē* (33) *wīn bycgan*, because the statement *iċ mæġ mē wīn bycgan* is false. Without the negation the indicative would be used: *iċ eom swā spēdiġ þæt iċ mæġ mē wīn bycgan*. So also after 'than', as in *þū spriċst* (41, 73) *dēoplicor þonne ūre ieldo* (19) *ā·beran mæge*, because the statement *ūre ieldo hit ā·beran mæġ* is false.

96. The subjunctive sometimes used illogically in statements of facts.

97. It is so used after such conjunctions as *ǣr* 'before', *oþ-þæt* 'until': *Bēowulf spræc* (76) *gielpword ǣr hē on będd stige*. Here Beowulf's going to bed, though a fact, is expressed with the subjunctive because at the time indicated by the principal clause it was not yet an accomplished fact.

98. Also with *þēah, þēah-þe* 'although': *þēah-þe hit wundorlić þynće, niht* (62) *nis nān-þing būtan þǣre eorþan sćeado.* Here the statement of the fact that it seems wonderful is put in the subjunctive to show that what is referred to ought not to seem wonderful because it is true.

Imperative.

99. The imperative singular of verbs with infinitive -*(a)n* can generally be formed by throwing off the infinitive ending, as in *heald!*, *sēć!*, *bēo!* from *healdan* 'hold', *sēćan* 'seek', *bēon* 'be'. In those with infinitive -*ian* it can be formed by throwing off the *þ* of the third singular, as in *fęre!* 'carry!' from *fęrian, hē fęreþ, ne sorga þū!* 'do not grieve!' from *sorgian, hē sorgaþ.*

100. But several verbs in -*an* preceded by double consonants have imperative in -*e* preceded by a single consonant, as in *sęle!* from *sęllan*, *sęġe* from *sęcgan.* So also some otherwise strong verbs, such as *sittan* 'sit', preterite *sæt*, imperative *site!*

101. The imperative plural is the same as the indicative present: *healdaþ, bēoþ, fęriaþ, wuniaþ, sęllaþ!*

Anomalous Verbs.

102. The following are the forms of the verb 'to be':—

		INDIC.	SUBJ.
Pres. Sing.	1.	*eom; bēo*	*sīe; bēo*
	2.	*eart; bist*	*sīe; bēo*
	3.	*is; biþ*	*sīe; bēo*
Plur.		*sind; bēoþ*	*sīen; bēon*

		INDIC.	SUBJ.
Pret. Sing.	1.	*wæs*	*wǣre*
	2.	*wǣre*	*wǣre*
	3.	*wæs*	*wǣre*
Plur.		*wǣron*	*wǣren*

Imper. *wes, wesaþ; bēo, bēoþ!*
Infin. *wesan, bēon.*

103. The following are the chief forms of *dōn* 'do' and *gān* 'go', both of which have weak preterites:—

Indic. Pres. Sing.	*iċ dō, hē dēþ*	*iċ gā, hē gǣþ*
Plur.	*dōþ*	*gāþ*
Pres.	*dyde*	*ēode*
Subj. Pres. Sing.	*dō*	*gā*
Plur.	*dōn*	*gān*
Pret.	*dyde*	*ēode*
Imper.	*dō, dōþ*	*gā, gāþ*
Particc.	*dōnde, ġedōn*	*gānde, ġegān*

104. The weak verb *habban* 'have' shows some irregularities:—

Indic. Pres. Sing.	*iċ hæbbe, þū hæfst, hē hæfþ*
Plur.	*habbaþ*
Pret.	*hæfde*
Subj. Pres.	*hæbbe*
Pret.	*hæfde*
Imper.	*hafa, habbaþ*

105. The verb *willan* 'will' resembles the preterite-present verbs, and shows a mixture of subjunctive forms in the present indicative:—

		INDIC.	SUBJ.
Pres. Sing.	1.	*iċ wile*	*wile*
	2.	*þū wilt*	*wile*
	3.	*hē wile*	*wile*
Plur.		*willaþ*	*willen*
Pret.		*wolde*	*wolde*

Tenses and Periphrastic Forms.

106. The future is often expressed by the present, as in *iċ ēow wīsiġe* 'I will show you the way', sometimes by 'will' and 'shall' as in Modern English. Of the two verbs 'to be' *bēon* is often used to express futurity, as in *iċ bēo sōna ġearo* (27) compared with *iċ eom ġearo*, or else continuity or repetition, as in *slǣp biþ dēaþe ġelīcost* (32).

107. The preterite has also the meaning of our perfect and pluperfect, which are however also expressed by periphrastic forms as in Modern English: *hīe habbaþ hine ofslæġen* 'they have killed him', *hīe hæfdon hine ofslæġen* 'they had killed him'. With intransitive verbs these tenses are generally formed with 'be', and the participle is then inflected so as to agree with the subject: *wē sind cumene, hīe wǣron cumene.*

108. The passive is sometimes formed with 'be', as in Modern English, in which case it generally implies a condition or state rather than an action, as in *þā wyrhtan wǣron ġesamnode.* When an action is implied *weorþan* (77) is used: *sēo wund ne wierþ* (106) *nǣfre ġehǣled* | *miċel dęmm wearþ ġedōn* | *maniġe męnn wurdon ofslæġene fram þǣm sǣmannum.* In the passive the participle agrees in gender and number with the subject.

Negation.

109. The negative particle is *ne*, which drops its vowel in many combinations, such as *n-ān* 'none', *n-ǣfre* 108, *neom* (95) 'am not', *neart* (93) 'art not', *nis* (98) 'is not', often with contractions and changes, as in *hē næs* 'was not', *hīe nǣron* 'were not', *iċ nyle* 'I will not', *hē nolde* 'would not', *hē nyste* 'knew not' compared with *wæs, wǣron, wile, wolde, wiste.*

110. *ne* is prefixed to the finite verb in a sentence and to all the other words in the sentence which admit of the contracted forms: *nān mann nyste nān þing* | *sēo wund ne wearþ nǣfre ġehǣled* (108). If there are no such words in the sentence, the *ne* is often strengthened by some such negative word as *nā* (92) 'not', *naht* 'nothing, not': *þæt hūs ne fēoll nā.*

TEXTS

Be þissum middanġearde.

Be þǣre sunnan.

1. Sēo sunne gǣþ betwēonan heofone and eorþan: on dæġ bufan eorþan, and on niht under þisse eorþan. Ǣfre hēo biþ iernende ymb þās eorþan, and ealswā leohte sċīnþ under þǣre eorþan on niht swā-swā hēo on dæġ dēþ bufan ūrum hēafdum.

2. On þā healfe þe hēo sċīnþ, þǣr biþ dæġ; and on þā healfe þe hēo ne sċīnþ, þǣr biþ niht.

3. Wē hātaþ ānne dæġ fram sunnan ūpgange oþ ǣfen. Fram þǣre sunnan ūpgange oþ-þæt hēo eft becume þǣr hēo ǣr ūp-stāg—on þǣm fæce sind ġetealde fēower and twentiġ tīda.

4. Sēo sunne is swiþe miċel: ealswā brād hēo is, þæs-þe bēċ sęcgaþ, swā eall eorþan ymbhwyrft. Ac hēo þynċþ ūs swiþe lȳtelu, forþǣmþe hēo is swiþe feorr fram ūrum ġesihþum.

5. Se mōna and ealle steorran on-fōþ leoht of þǣre miċlan sunnan.

Be þǣre nihte.

6. Niht is ġesętt mannum tō ręste on þissum middanġearde. Þēah-þe hit wundorliċ þynċe, nis niht nān-þing būtan þǣre eorþan sċeado betwēonan þǣre sunnan and mancynne.

Be þǣm mōnan.

7. Dæġhwǣmlīċe þæs mōnan leoht biþ weaxende and waniende. Simle hē węnt his hrycg tō þǣre sunnan.

Be þǣm ġēare.

8. On þǣm ġēare sind ġetealde twelf mōnþas, and twā and fiftiġ wucena, þrēo hund daga and fīf and siextiġ daga, and þǣr-tō·ēacan siex tīda.

Be reġne.

9. Reġnas cumaþ of þǣre lyfte. Sēo lyft ā·tīehþ þone wǣtan of ealre eorþan and of þǣre sǣ and ġegaderaþ tō scūrum; and þonne hēo māre ā·beran ne mæġ, þonne fielþ hit of·dūne.

10. Hagol cymþ of þǣm reġndropum, þonne hīe bēoþ ġefrorene uppe on þǣre lyfte, and swā sōna feallaþ, swā-swā sum sċop be him ġieddode:

Hagol biþ ·hwītost corna; hwierfþ hit of ·heofones lyfte,
wealcaþ hit ·windes scūras; wierþ hit tō ·wætere siþþan.

Be þǣre lyfte.

11. Þēos lyft þe wē on libbaþ is ān þāra fēower ġesċeafta. Nis nān þing þe næbbe þā fēower ġesċeafta him mid: þæt is lyft, and fȳr, and eorþe, and wæter.

12. Lyft is swīþe þynne. Sēo ofer·gǣþ ealne middanġeard, and ūp-āstīġþ oþ þone mōnan. On þǣre flēogaþ fuglas swā-swā fisċas swimmaþ on wætere. Ne mihte hira nān flēogan, nǣre sēo lyft þe hīe bierþ. Sēo lyft ā·bierþ eall wolcnu and ealle stormas.

13. Sēo lyft, þonne hēo ā·styred is, biþ wind.

Be manna cræftum.

14. Hwelċne cræft canst þū?
Iċ eom munuc.
15. Hwæt cunnon þās þīne ġefēran?
Sume sind ierþlingas, sume sċēaphierdas, sume hrīþerhierdas, sume huntan, sume fisċeras, sume fugleras, sume ċīepemęnn, sume sċōwyrhtan, sume sealteras, sume bæceras.

Se ierþling.

16. Hwæt sęġst þū, ierþling? Hū begǣst þū þinne cræft?
Lā lēof, þearle iċ swince! Ǣlċe dæġe iċ sċeal on dæġred ūt-gān. Þonne sċeal iċ þā oxan tō felda drīfan and tō þǣre sylh ġeocian. Nis nān winter swā stearc þæt iċ dyrre æt hām lūtian: ne dearr iċ for mīnes hlāfordes ęġe. Ac þonne iċ þā oxan ġeġeocod hæbbe, and þæt sċear and þone culter on þǣre sylh ġefæstnod hæbbe, þonne sċeal iċ fulne æcer ęrian oþþe māre.
17. Hæfst þū ǣniġne ġefēran?
Ġiese, iċ hæbbe cnapan: sē sċeal þā oxan mid gāde þīen. Sē is nū hās for ċiele and hrēame.
18. Hwæt māre dēst þū? Hæfst þū ġiet māre tō dōnne?
Ġiese lēof, miċel iċ hæbbe tō dōnne! Iċ sċeal þāra oxena binne mid hīeġe ā-fyllan, and hīe wæterian, and hira steall feormian.
19. Ēalā, þæt is miċel ġedeorf!
Ġiese lēof, hit is miċel ġedeorf, for-þǣmþe iċ neom frseo.

Se sċēaphierde.

20. Hwæt sęġst þū, sċēaphierde? Hæfst þū ǣniġ ġedeorf?

Ġiese lēof, iċ hæbbe miċel ġedeorf! On ǣrnemerġen iċ drīfe mīn sċēap tō lǣswe. Siþþan stande iċ ofer hīe mid hundum, þȳ·lǣsþe wulfas hīe for·swelgen. Þonne on ǣfen iċ lǣde hīe on-ġēan tō hira locum. Iċ hīe melce tuwa on dæġe. Iċ maciġe buteran and ċiese. And iċ eom mīnum hlāforde ġetrīewe.

Se hrīþerhierde.

21. Ēalā hrīþerhierde, hwæt dēst þū?

Lā lēof, iċ swince þearle! Þonne se ierþling þā oxan on·ġeocaþ, þonne lǣde iċ hīe tō lǣswe; and ealle niht iċ stande ofer hīe, waciende for þēofum; and þæs on morgenne iċ hīe betǣċe eft þǣm ierþlinge, wel ġefylde and ġewæterode.

Se hunta.

22. Is þes mann ān of þīnum ġefērum?

Ġiese.

23. Canst þū ǣniġ þing?

Anne cræft iċ cann.

24. Hwelċne cræft canst þū?

Iċ eom hunta.

25. Hwæs hunta eart þū?

Iċ eom þæs cyninges hunta.

26. Hū begǣst þū þīnne cræft?

Iċ breġde mē nętt, and ā·sętte hīe on ġehæpre stōwe. Þonne tyhte iċ mīne hundas þæt hīe þāra wildēora ehten, oþ-þæt hīe on unġearwe on þā nętt becumen. Þonne hīe þus ġelæht sind, þonne cume iċ tō, and hīe on þǣm nęttum of·slēa.

27. Ne canst þū būtan nęttum huntian?

Ġiese, iċ cann būtan nęttum huntian.

28. Hū?

Iċ fō þā wildēor mid swiftum hundum.

29. Hwelċ wildēor ġefēhst þū swīþost?

Iċ ġefō heorotas, and rān, and bāras, and hwīlum haran.

30. Wǣre þū tō·dæġ on huntoþe?

Nese, for·þǣm hit is sunnan-dæġ; ac ġiestrandæġ iċ wæs on huntoþe.

31. Hwæt ġefēnge þū?

Iċ ġefēng twēġen heorotas and ānne bār.

32. Hū ġefēnge þū hīe?

Þā heorotas on nęttum iċ ġefēng, and þone bār iċ of·sticode.

33. Hū wǣre þū swā ġedyrstiġ þæt þū bār of·sticodest?

Þā hundas hine bedrifon tō mē, and iċ þǣr fæstlīċe on·ġēan-stōd, and hine fǣrlīċe mid spere of·sticode.

34. Swīþe ġedyrstiġ wǣre þū þā!

Ne sċeal hunta forhtmōd bēon, for·þǣm missenlicu wildēor wuniaþ on wudum.

35. Hwæt dēst þū ymb þīnne huntoþ?

Iċ sęlle þǣm cyninge swā hwæt swā iċ ġefō, for·þǣm iċ eom his hunta.

36. Hwæt sęlþ hē þē?

Hē sċrȳtt mē wel and fētt, and hwīlum hē mē hors sęlþ oþþe bēag, þæt iċ þȳ ġeornor mīnne cræft begā.

Se fisċere.

37. Hwelċne cræft canst þū?

Iċ eom fisċere.

38. Hwæt beġietst þū of þīnum cræfte?

Bīleofan iċ mē beġiete, and sċrūd, and feoh.

39. Hū ġefēhst þū þā fisċas?

Iċ gā on mīnne bāt, and rōwe ūt on þā ēa, and weorpe mīn nętt on þā ēa. Hwīlum iċ weorpe angel ūt mid ǣse, oþþe spyrtan; and swā hwæt swā hīe ġehæftaþ iċ nime.

40. Hwæt dēst þū ġif hit unclǣne fisċas bēoþ?

Iċ weorpe þā unclǣnan ūt, and nime þā clǣnan mē tō męte.

41. Hwǣr ċīepst þū þīne fisċas?

On þǣre ċeastre.

42. Hwā byġþ hīe?

Þā ċeasterware. Ne mæġ iċ hira swā fela ġefōn swā iċ sęllan mæġe.

43. Hwelċe fisċas ġefēhst þū?

Ǣlas, and hacodas, and sċēotan, and ealle ōþre fisċas þe on þǣm ēam swimmaþ.

44. For·hwȳ ne fisċast þū on sǣ?

Hwīlum iċ dō swā, ac seldon; for·þǣm hit is mē miċel rēwett tō þǣre sǣ.

45. Hwæt ġefēhst þū on þǣre sǣ?

Hæringas, and leaxas, and styrian, and lopestran, and crabban, and fela ōþerra fisċa.

46. Wilt þū hwæl fōn?

Niċ!

47. For·hwȳ?

For·þǣm miċel pleoh is þæt man hwæl ġefō. Lǣsse pleoh mē biþ þæt iċ tō þǣre ēa gā mid mīnum bāte þonne iċ mid manigum sċipum on hwælhuntoþ fare.

48. For·hwȳ swā?

For·þǣm mē is lēofre þæt iċ fisċ ġefō þe iċ of·slēan mæġ þonne iċ fisċ ġefō þe nealles þæt ān mē selfne ac ēac swelċe mīne ġefēran mid ānum słęġe besęnċan mæġ oþþe of·slēan.

49. And þēah maniġe ġefōþ hwalas, and þǣm frēċennessum æt·berstaþ, and miċelne sċeatt þanon beġietaþ.

Sōþ þū sęġst; ac iċ ne dearr for mīnes mōdes slǣwþe.

Se fuglere.

50. Hwæt sęġst þū, fuglere? Hū beswīcst þū þā fuglas?

Iċ hīe on maniġfealde wīsan beswīce: hwīlum mid nęttum, hwīlum mid grīnum, hwīlum mid træppum, hwīlum mid līme, hwīlum mid wistlunge, hwīlum mid hafoce.

51. Hæfst þū hafocas?

Ġiese.

52. Canst þū tęmian hafocas?

Ġiese, iċ cann: hū sċeolden hīe mē nytte bēon, būtan iċ hīe tęmian cūþe?

53. Sęle mē hafoc!

Iċ þē sęlle lustlīċe, ġif þū mē sęlst swiftne hund. Hwelċne hafoc wilt þū habban, þone māran hwæþer-þe þone læssan?

54. Sęle mē þone māran! Hū ā·fētst þū þīne hafocas?

Hīe hīe selfe fēdaþ on wintra ġe ēac swelċe mē, and on lęnċtene iċ hīe læte tō wuda æt·flēogan; and iċ mē nime briddas on hærfest and hīe ġetęmiġe.

55. For·hwȳ lætst þū þā ġetęmedan hafocas þē æt·flēogan?

For·þǣm iċ nyle hīe on sumera fēdan, for·þǣmþe hīe þearle etaþ.

56. Ac maniġe fēdaþ þā ġetęmedan ofer sumor, þæt hīe hīe eft ġearwe hæbben.

Ġiese, hīe dōþ swā. Ac iċ nyle on swelċum ġeswince mid him bēon, for·þǣm iċ cann ōþre ġefōn—nealles ānne, ac maniġe.

Se mangere.

57. Hwæt sęġst þū, mangere?

Iċ sęcge þæt iċ eom swīþe nytt þǣm cyninge, and þǣm ealdormannum, and þǣm weliġum, and eallum folce.

58. Hū?

Iċ ā·stīge on mīn sċip mid mīnum hlæstum, and fare ofer

sǣ, and sęlle mīn þing, and bycge dēorwierþu þing þe on þissum lande ā·cenned ne bēoþ; and iċ hit lǣde tō ēow hider ofer sǣ mid miċlum plēo; and hwīlum iċ þoliġe for·lidennesse, swā þæt mē losiaþ eall mīn þing, and iċ self unēaþe cucu æt·berste.

59. Hwelċ þing lǣtst þū ūs hider ofer sǣ?

Pællas, seoloc, seldcūþ rēaf, wyrtġemang, wīn, ele, elpendbān, dēorwierþe ġimmas, gold, tin, mæstling, ār, seolfor, glæs, and fela ōþerra þinga.

60. Wilt þū þīn þing hēr on lande sęllan wiþ þǣm ilcan weorþe þe þū hīe þǣr ūte mid ġebohtest?

Niċ; hwæt fręmede mē þonne mīn ġedeorf? Ac iċ wile hīe wiþ māran weorþe hēr sęllan þonne iċ hīe þǣr mid ġebohte, þæt iċ mæġe mē sum ġestrēon beġietan, þe iċ mē mid ā·fēdan mæġe and mīn wīf and mīn bearn.

Se sċōwyrhta.

61. Þū sċōwyrhta, hwæt wyrċst þū ūs tō nytte?

Mīn cræft is ēow swīþe nytt and swīþe nīedbehēfe. Iċ bycge hȳda and fell, and hīe ġearciġe mid mīnum cræfte, and wyrċe þǣr-of missenliċes cynnes ġesċȳ, leþerhosa, þwangas, ġerǣdu, flasċan, and fǣtelsas; and ne mæġ ēower nān ofer wihter wunian būtan mīnum cræfte.

Se sealtere.

62. Ēalā þū sealtere, hwæt fręmeþ ūs þīn cræft?

Mīn cræft fręmeþ ēow eallum þearle. Ne mæġ ēower nān flǣsċmętta brūcan būtan mīnum cræfte. Hwelċ mann mæġ swētmętta brūcan būtan sealtes swæcce? Hwā ġefylþ his cleofan and hēdærn būtan mīnum cræfte? Ēowru butere eall ēow losaþ and ēower ċiese būtan iċ hīe mid mīnum cræfte ġehealde. Ne ġē ne magon furþum ēowerra wyrta brūcan būtan mē.

Se bæcere.

63. Hwæt sęġst þū, bæcere? Hwǣm fręmeþ þīn cræft? Hwæþer mæġen wē būtan þē ūre līf ā·drēogan?

Tō hwīle ġē magon ēower līf ā·drēogan būtan mīnum cræfte, ac nā lange ne tō wel; for·þǣm būtan mīnum cræfte ǣlċ bēod biþ ǣmettiġ ġeþuht, and būtan hlāfe ǣlċ męte biþ tō wlǣttan ġehwierfed. Iċ ġestrangiġe manna heortan: iċ eom wera mæġen; ġe furþum þā lȳtlingas nyllaþ mē for·bolian.

Se cōc.

64. Hwæt sęcge wē be þǣm cōce? Hwæþer wē his cræftes tō āwihte beþurfon?

Ġif ġē mē of ēowrum ġefērsċipe ūt-ādrīfaþ, ġē etaþ ēowre wyrta grēne and ēowre flǣsċmęttas hrēawe; ne magon ġē furþum fǣtt broþ habban būtan mīnum cræfte.

65. Ne ręċċe wē be þīnum cræfte: nis hē ūs nā nīedbehēfe, for·þǣm wē magon selfe sēoþan þā þing þe tō sēoþanne sind, and brǣdan þā þing þe tō brǣdanne sind.

Ġif ġē mē ūt-ādrīfaþ and þus dōþ, þonne bēo ġē ealle þēowas, and nān ēower ne biþ hlāford; and þēah·hwæþre ġē ne magon etan būtan mīnum cræfte.

Þā ōþre wyrhtan.

66. Ēalā munuc, iċ ġesēo þē habban gōde ġefēran and swīþe nytte; hæfst þū ōþre ēac him?

Iċ hæbbe īsensmiþas, goldsmiþas, seolforsmiþas, trēowwyrhtan, and maniġe ōþre.

67. Hæfst þū wīsne ġeþeahtere?

Ġewisslīċe iċ hæbbe: hū mæġ ūre ġefērsċipe bēon ġewissod būtan ġeþeahtere?

68. Ēalā þū wīsa ġeþeahtere, hwæt sęġst þū? Hwelċ þissa cræfta is þē fyrmest ġeþuht?

Iċ þē sęcge, Godes þēowdōm is mē fyrmest ġeþuht betweox þissum cræftum, swā-swā Crīst on his godspelle cwæþ 'Fyrmest sēċaþ Godes rīċe, and þās þing eall ēow bēoþ tō-ġeīeċed'.

69. And hwelċ woruldcræft is þē fyrmest ġeþuht?

Eorþtilþ; for-þǣm se ierþling fētt ūs ealle.

70. (Se smiþ sęġþ:) Hwanon hæfþ se ierþling sċear oþþe culter, oþþe furþum gāde, būtan of mīnum cræfte? Hwanon hæfþ se fisċere angel, oþþe se sċōwyrhta āwel, oþþe se sēamere nǣdle būtan of mīnum ġeweorce?

71. (Se ġeþeahtere andswaraþ:) Sōþ þū sęġst; ac ūs eallum lēofre is mid þǣm ierþlinge tō wīcianne þonne mid þē: for·þǣm se ierþling sęlþ ūs hlāf and drynċe; ac þū, hwæt sęlst þū ūs on þīnre smiþþan būtan īsene spearcan, and bēatendra slęcga swēġ and blāwendra byliġa?

72. (Se trēowwyrhta sęġþ:) Hwelċ ēower ne notaþ mīnes cræftes, þonne iċ ēow eallum hūs wyrċe and sċipu and missenlicu fatu?

73. (Se smiþ andswaraþ:) Ēalā trēowwyrhta, for·hwȳ spriċst þū swā, þonne furþum ān þȳrel þū ne miht dōn būtan mīnum cræfte?

74. (Se ġeþeahtere sęġþ:) Ēalā ġefēran and gōde wyrhtan, uton hrædlīċe ġesēman þās ġeflitu, and sīe sibb and ġeþwǣrnes betweox ēow, and fręmme ǣlċ ōþrum on his cræfte! And uton weorþian þone ierþling, of þǣm wē beġietaþ ūs selfum bīleofan and fōdor ūrum horsum! And iċ ġelǣre eallum wyrhtum þisne rǣd: þæt ānra-ġehwelċ his cræft ġeornlīċe begā. For·þǣm sē-þe his cræft for·lǣtt, sē biþ fram þǣm cræfte for·lǣten. Swā hwelċ swā þū sīe, swā mæssepreōst, swā munuc, swā ċeorl, swā cęmpa, begā ġeornlīċe þīnne

cræft! And bēo þæt þæt þū eart! For·þǣm hit is miċel dęmm and miċel sċand ġif man nyle bēon þæt þæt hē is and þæt þæt hē bēon sċeal.

Se munuc.

75. Ēalā ġē ċild, hū līcaþ ēow þēos sprǣc?

Wel hēo ūs līcaþ; ac þearle dēoplīċe þū spriċst and ofer ūre mǣþ. Ac sprec wiþ ūs æfter ūrum andġiete, þæt wē mæġen under·standan þā þing þe þū spriċst.

76. Iċ āsċiġe ēow 'For·hwȳ leorniġe ġē swā ġeornlīċe?'

For·þǣm wē nyllaþ bēon swā-swā stunt nīetenu, þe nān þing nyton būtan gærs and wæter.

77. Hwæt wille ġē þonne bēon?

Wē willaþ wīse bēon.

78. On hwelċum wīsdōme? Wille ġē lytiġe bēon and fācenfulle, wel-sprecende and yfel-þęnċende, swā-swā byrġels, þe is wiþ·ūtan fæġer and wiþ·innan fūl?

Wē nyllaþ swā bēon wīse; for·þǣm sē nis nā wīs sē-þe hine selfne mid līcettunge beswīcþ.

79. Hū wille ġē bēon wīse?

Wē willaþ bilewite bēon būtan līcettunge, and wīse, þæt wē mæġen yfel for·būgan and gōd dōn. Þēah·hwæþre ġiet þū spriċst wiþ ūs dēoplicor þonne ūre ieldo ā·beran mæġe. Ac sprec wiþ ūs æfter ūrum ġewunan, næs swā dēoplīċe.

80. Iċ wile dōn ealswā ġē biddaþ. Þū cnapa, hwæt dydest þū tō·dæġ?

Maniġ þing iċ dyde. On þisse niht, þā-þā iċ þone cnyll ġehīerde, þā ā·rās iċ of mīnum będde, and tō ċiriċan ēode, and sang uhtsang mid þǣm ġebrōþrum. Æfter þǣm wē sungon 'be eallum hālgum' and lofsangas. Æfter þissum prīm wē sungon and seofon sealmas, mid letānian and capitolmæssan, and siþþan underntīd and þæs dæġes mæssan.

Æfter þissum wē sungon middæġ, and ǣton, and druncon, and slēpon; and eft wē ā·rison, and sungon nōn. And nū wē sind hēr beforan þē, ġearwe tō ġehīeranne hwæt þū ūs sęcgan wilt.

81. Hwonne wille ġē ǣfensang singan oþþe nihtsang?

Þonne hit tīma biþ.

82. Wǣre þū beswungen tō·dæġ?

Nese; for·þǣm iċ mē wærlīċe hēold.

83. And hū þīne ġefēran?

Hwæt āsċast þū mē be þǣm? Ne dearr iċ þē ūre dīeġelnessa yppan; ūre ġehwelċ wāt ġif hē beswungen wæs oþþe nā.

84. Hwæt itst þū?

Wyrta, and ǣġru, and fisċ, and ċīese, and buteran, and bēana, and eall clǣnu þing iċ ete mid miċelre þancunge. Ne brūce iċ ġīet flǣsċmętta, for·þǣm iċ eom ċild under ġierde drohtiende.

85. Swīþe ġīfre eart þū, þonne þū eall þing itst þe þē beforan ġesętt sind.

Neom iċ swā miċel swelgere þæt iċ mæġe ealra cynna męttas on ānum mǣle etan. Hwīlum iċ brūce ānes cynnes mętes, hwīlum ōþres, for·þǣm iċ neom nā swelgere.

86. Hwæt drincst þū?

Iċ drince ealo, ġif iċ hit hæbbe; oþþe wæter, ġif iċ ealo næbbe.

87. Ne drincst þū wīn?

Neom iċ swā spēdiġ þæt iċ mæġe mē wīn bycgan; and wīn nis nā ċilda drynċe ne dysiġra, ac ealdra and wīsra.

88. Hwǣr slǣpst þū?

On þǣm slǣpærne mid þǣm ġebrōþrum.

89. Hwā ā·węċþ þē tō uhtsange?

Hwīlum iċ ġehīere þone cnyll, and ā·rīse; hwīlum mīn lārēow ā·węċþ mē stīþlīċe mid ġierde.

---

90. And nū, ġē ċild, iċ ēow maniġe þæt ġē þǣm godcundum lārum ġehīersumien and ġerisenlīċe ġebǣren on ǣlċre stōwe. Þonne ġē ġehīeraþ þǣre ċiriċan bellan, gāþ þēawlīċe tō ġebede, and būgaþ ēaþmōdlīċe tō þǣm hālgum wēofodum, and standaþ ġerisenlīċe, and singaþ ānmōdlīċe, and ġebiddaþ for ēowrum synnum, and gāþ ūt būtan hyġelēaste tō claustre oþþe tō leornunge.

Bēowulfes sīþ.

Be Hrōþgāre, Dęna cyninge.

91. Hit ġelamp ġēo þæt ān cyning wæs on Dęnum, sē wæs hāten Hrōþgār. And se Hrōþgār wæs mǣre hęretoga, swā þæt his māgas him ġeorne ġehīerdon, oþ-þæt his folgoþ wēox þearle, and hē hæfde siġe swā hwider swā hē ēode, ǣġþer ġe on sǣ ġe on lande.

92. And sōna swā hē tō rīċe fēng, swā ġesamnode hē miċle fierd, and his fīend ġesohte on hira āgnum landum, and hīe swīþe for·slōg and for·dyde, oþ hīe ealle unġemetliċne ęġe fram him hæfdon.

93. Þā sęndon hīe him ǣrendracan tō, and hine friþes bǣdon. And hē him þæs ġetīþode on þæt ġerād þæt hīe him gafol gulden, and hine him tō hlāforde ġecuren. And hīe þæt ġelǣston swā; and hīe him ġīslas sealdon and miċle āþas; and man þā fulne frēondsċipe ġefæstnode mid worde and mid wędde on ǣġþre healfe.

94. Þā þæt gafol ġelǣst wæs and friþāþas ā·sworene wǣron, þā węnde Hrōþgār cyning on·ġēan tō Dęnum; and hīe his ġefæġene wǣron. And hē hēold siþþan his rīċe on gōdre ġeþwǣrnesse and on miċelre sibbe.

Hū Hrōþgār ġetimbrede Heorot.

95. Þā be·arn him on mōde þæt hē miċle healle timbrede, and þǣr·inne his mannum ġedǣlde ealle þā hęrehȳþ þe hīe ǣr ġefēngon.

96. Þā hēt hē ealle þā bętstan wyrhtan tō his cynestōle ġebannan, ǣġþer ġe of his āgnum rīċe ġe of eallum þǣm þēodum þe him under·þīedde wǣron. Þā þā wyrhtan ealle ġesamnode wǣron, þā wearþ þæt weorc on·gunnen.

97. Þā ġelamp hit æfter fierste þæt sēo heall ġearo wæs. Sēo wæs ealra hūsa mǣst, and fæġerost on tō lōcianne. Hē þā Hrōþgār cyning ā·scōp hire naman 'Heorot'.

98. Ne ā·lēag hē nā his bēot; ac hē ġesamnode ealle his męnn tō miċlum ġebēorsċipe on þǣre healle, and him eall ġedǣlde þe hē ahte ġe on seolfre ġe on golde ġe on eallum māþmum.

99. Þǣr man mihte þā ġesēon blisse on Heorote þǣr man eft ġeseah þā mǣstan iermþe. Þǣr mihte man þǣre hearpan swēġ ġehīeran and þæs sċopes sang. Hē sang be frumsċeafte: hū se ælmihtiga eorþan worhte and þā wæteru þe hīe ūtan ymb·licgaþ; and hū hē sunnan and mōnan on heofone ġesętte, mannum tō leohte; and hū hē þā eorþan mid trēowum frætwode and mid gærse and mid eallum wyrtum; and hū hē līf sealde eallum cucum wihtum þe þā eorþan ġeond·hweorfaþ.

Be Gręndle.

100. On þisse blisse þurh·wunode Hrōþgār cyning and his męnn lange tīd, oþ-þæt him fēond onsǣġe wearþ. Þæt wæs unfǣlu wiht, Gręndel hātte. Sē būde on þǣm mearclande, and hæfde him fæsten ġeworht on fęnnum, on·middan þǣm sweartum mōrum.

101. Sume męnn cwǣdon þæt Gręndel wǣre of Cāines cynne. For·þǣm, þā Cāin of·slōg Ābel his brōþor, þā wearþ him se ælmihtiga gram, and hine on wræcsīþ ā·sęnde, and hēt hine on wēstenne wunian, feorr mancynne. Þanon on·wōcon ealle unfǣle wihta, dweorgas, and ielfe, and eotenas, þe wiþ God wunnon.

102. Þā ne mihte Gręndel þolian þæt hē ǣlċe dæġe

blisse ġehīerde on Heorote, and hē self ūte wunode on þīestrum.

103. Þā on niht æfter þǣm ġebēorsċipe, þā þā męnn slēpon on þǣre healle, þā wearþ se rēþa Gręndel sōna ġearo: hē him on unġearwe on-bestæl, þā hīe him nānes yfeles ne wēndon, and hira þrītiġ ġenam, and mid him fęrede hām tō his fæstenne, þǣre hęrehȳþe fæġniende; for·þǣm hit wæs his þēaw þæt hē hlāf ne ǣt, ne wæter ne dranc, ac ǣt manna līchaman and hira blōd dranc.

104. Þā þæs on morgenne wearþ Gręndles hęrġung eallum mannum cūþ. Þā wæs miċel wōp ā·hafen and miċel hēofung. And se gōda cyning Hrōþgār sæt unblīþe, and him wæs wāniende ǣġþer ġe his āgne heardsǣlþa ġe ealles þæs folces.

105. Þā wæs Gręndles spor sweotole ġesīene. Ac næs þāra nān þe hit ġespyrian dorste: wæs him se fēond tō strang.

106. Ne lēt Gręndel nā langne fierst þæt hē eft ne cōm, ac ymb āne niht māran wælsliht ġefręmede: ne mearn hē for þǣre fǣhþe.

107. Þā nolde nān mann lęnġ wunian on Heorote on niht, ac hīe sohton him ęlleshwǣr ręste on ōþrum būrum, oþ-þæt Heorot stōd ǣmettiġ, eallum mannum unnytt, and on þǣm þurh·wunode twelf winter.

108. Ne wēne iċ þæt ǣniġ mann ā·tęllan mæġe ealne þone dęmm þe Dęnum ġedōn wearþ on þǣm twelf ġēarum. Tō·ēacan þǣm maniġfealdum yflum þe hīe drēogende wǣron, ne þorfton þā māgas þāra of·slæġenra nānre bōte wēnan æt Gręndles handum: hē nolde nā ġeþingian wiþ hīe, ne þā fǣhþe mid fēo for·ġieldan, swā riht biþ.

109. Wæs þæt miċel wundor þæt Gręndel āna wiþ hīe ealle winnende wæs! On eallum þǣm fæce hē rīċsode on

Heorote on þǣm sweartum nihtum swelċe hē cyning wǣre; būtan hē ne dorste nā þæt cynesetl grētan for Godes ęġe. Ac ǣlċe dæġe, sōna þæs hit dagode, ġewāt hē eft ofer þā wildan mōras his fæsten sēċan. Ac nān ne dorste him æfter-spyrian.

110. Þā wæs swā miċel ęġe fram Gręndle þæt nān mann ne mihte ā·þęnċan ne ā·cræftan hū hīe him wiþ·standan mihten, oþþe Dęna eard wiþ hine ġehealdan. Þā on·gann Hrōþgār cyning ġeorne tō smēaganne wiþ his witan hwæt him eallum rǣdlicost þuhte, þæt man Dęna earde ġebeorgan mihte, ǣr hē mid ealle for·dōn wurde.

111. Þā hīe þā ġesāwon þæt him nāhwæþer ne dohte, ne wīg ne wīsdōm, þā ġerǣddon þā witan þæt hīe hira godum blōten æt hira heargum æfter hǣþenum ġewunan, þæt hīe him sume helpe ġefręmeden. And nā þȳ lǣs for eallum þissum ġeblōte hē fērde swā hē self wolde, and þæt earme folc slōg and hīende.

112. Þā on·gunnon þā sċopas lēoþ wyrċan be þǣm, oþ-þæt hit wearþ on eallum norþlandum cūþ hū Dęne ġebrocode wǣron.

Be Bēowulfe.

113. Þā wæs þǣr sum þēod on Swēolande þe man hǣtt Ġēatas; Hyġelāc wæs ġehāten hira cyning. Sē hæfde þeġn, þæs nama wæs Bēowulf; sē wæs þæs cyninges nefa. And se Bēowulf wæs ealra manna cēnost and stręnġest. Is þæt ġesæġd þæt hē hæfde þrītiġra manna mæġen on his hand-gripe.

114. Þā wurdon Gręndles undǣda ēac on Ġēatum cūþe. And hraþe þæs-þe Bēowulf þæt ġehīerde, swā hēt hē him sċip ġierwan: cwæþ þæt hē wolde Hrōþgār sēċan, þā him wæs manna þearf. And hē him ġeċēas fīftīene cęmpan, þā cēnostan þe hē findan mihte, þæt hīe on þǣm sīþe his ġefēran wǣren.

115. Hē ēode þā mid his ġefērum tō þǣre sǣ strande, þǣr hē his sċip wiste. Hīe þā þæt sċip ūt-sċufon, and selfe on ēodon mid hira hęreġeatwum. Þā sętton hīe þā seġlas; and hīe hæfdon ambyrne wind, and hīe wǣron ealne þone dæġ iernende under seġle. Þā on niht hīe ġewīcodon. And þæs on morgenne hīe siġldon furþor, oþ-þæt hīe clifu ġesāwon him beforan, swelċe hwītne weall.

116. Þā wiston hīe þæt hīe tō Dęna lande cumene wǣron. Þā tugon hīe hira sċip ūp on þæt sand, and bǣron hira wǣpnu ūt. Þā stōdon hīe on þǣm strande, Gode þanciende þæs-þe hē hīe ġesunde þider brohte.

Be þǣm wearde.

117. Þā wæs þǣr sum cyninges þeġn, sē wæs tō þǣm ġesętt þæt hē sċolde sǣwearde healdan. Sē of þǣm clife ġeseah þæt sċip tō lande cuman, and þā męnn ūp-gān mid wǣpnum mid ealle. Þā bræc hine firwit hwæt þā męnn wǣren.

118. Þā rād hē niþer tō þǣm strande, and his spere ā·cweahte, and him þus tō-cwæþ, swīþe unforht: 'Hwæt sind ġē þe þus ġewǣpnode hider on land cōmon on ēowrum langsċipe? Iċ eom Hrōþgāres þeġn, Dęna cyninges; iċ eom tō þǣm ġesętt þæt iċ sǣwearde healde, and þisne eard węriġe, þȳ·læsþe sċiphęre ūs on unġearwe on-bestele. Nǣfre ne dorste ūrra fēonda nān openlīċe hider on land cuman.'

119. Þā cwæþ hē eft: 'Ne ġeseah iċ nǣfre māran mann þonne ēower sum is: þǣm ġerīst wel þæt hē wǣpnu bere, būtan him his ansīen lēoge! Ac nū iċ sċeal witan hwanon ġē cumene sind, ǣr ġē furþor ūp-gān þæt land tō sċēawianne.

Nū ġē sǣmęnn, ġehīeraþ mīnne ānfealdne ġeþoht: ofost is bętst tō cȳþanne hwanon ġē cumene sind.'

120. Him þā Bēowulf andswarode, and þus cwæþ: 'Wē sind Hyġelāces þeġnas, Ġēata cyninges. Mīn fæder wæs on eallum folcum cūþ, sē wæs Ęcgþēow hāten, æþeles cynnes mann. Þurh holdne hyġe wē sind hider cumene þīnne hlāford sēċan, Hrōþgār cyning. Wē habbaþ miċel ǣrende tō þǣm cyninge. Þū wāst ġif hit swā is swā wē sęcgan ġehīerdon; þæt sum dīeġle fēond unāsęcgendliċ yfel fręmeþ on Dęnum, mid·þǣmþe hē hīe of·slihþ and for·swilġþ on þǣm þīestrum nihtum. Iċ mæġ Hrōþgār cyning rǣd ġelǣran, hū hē þone fēond ofer·swīþan mæġe, ġif him se ælmihtiga þæs ġetīþaþ þæt him eft bōt cume þāra yfla þe him onsǣġu sind.'

121. Þā cwæþ se weard: 'Gōdum þeġne ġedafenaþ þæt hē þæt ġesċād wite worda and dǣda! Iċ þæt ġehīere þæt þis is hold werod Dęna cyninge. Ġewītaþ nū mid ēowrum wǣpnum Hrōþgār sēċan; iċ ēow wīsiġe. Swelċe ēac iċ mīnum mannum bebēode þæt hīe ēower sċip wiþ ealle fīend ġehealden, oþ-þæt hit ēow eft bierþ ofer sǣ tō Ġēata lande, swelċum ēower ġifeþe biþ þæt hīe him ġesunde beorgaþ.'

Hū Ġēatas tō Heorote cōmon.

122. Hīe þā lēton hira sċip him behindan, on ancre fæst: ġewiton him selfe forþ on hira hęreġeatwum. Hīe hæfdon hira helmas on hēafdum. On þǣm helmum wǣron eofera līc, of golde ġeworht. Þā anliċnessa wǣron tō þǣm ġeworhte þæt hīe þāra manna fēorum wiþ ǣlċe frēcennesse ġeburgen.

123. Hīe þā ēodon forþ oþ-þæt hīe þā healle ġesāwon þe ealra hūsa mǣrost wæs; wæs se hrōf mid golde ġefrætwod, of þǣm leoht sċān ofer maniġ land. Hē þā se weard him þæt ġiesthūs ġetǣhte, þæt hīe mihten hīe ġeręstan. Þā ġewęnde hē his hors, and him tō cwæþ: 'Mǣl is mē tō feranne. Ġehealde ēow se ælmihtiga ġesunde on ēowrum siþe! Iċ tō sǣ wile, þæt iċ wiþ unfriþhęre wearde healde.'

124. Hīe þā be þǣre stānstrǣte ēodon, oþ-þæt hīe tō þǣm ġiesthūse cōmon. Hīe þā ā·lęġdon hira sċieldas wiþ þæs hūses weall, and sętton hira speru on ānre hyrnan eall æt·samne. Þā ēodon hīe tō þǣm bęnċum þæt hīe hīe ġeręsten, for·þǣm hīe wǣron wēriġe æfter þǣre sǣfare.

125. Þā wæs þǣr sum mann, Wulfgār·hātte, wīs mann and gōd cęmpa, sē him tō cwæþ: 'Hwanon cume ġē þus ġewǣpnode hider on Dęna land? Iċ eom Hrōþgāres ǣrendraca. Ne ġeseah iċ nǣfre swā mōdiġe męnn hider on land cuman! Wēn is þæt ġē for mǣrþe Hrōþgār sohton, nealles for wræcsīþe!'

126. Þā andswarode him Bēowulf: 'Wē sind Hyġelāces þeġnas, Ġēata cyninges. Bēowulf is mīn nama. Iċ wile Hrōþgāre cyninge mīn ǣrende sęcgan, ġif hē for his gōdnesse ġeunnan wile þæt wē hine grētan mōten.'

127. Þā cwæþ Wulfgār: 'Iċ wile Hrōþgāre cyninge þīn ǣrende ā·bēodan, swā þū biddende eart, and þē þā andsware þǣr·rihte ġecȳþan.'

128. Hē þā ēode hrædlīċe þǣr se cyning sæt mid his ealdormannum, and ġestōd beforan þæs cyninges eaxlum, swā þeġnes riht biþ, and him þus tō cwæþ: 'Hēr sind feorrancumene męnn of Ġēata þēode, Bēowulf hātte hira lāttēow. Hīe biddende sind þæt hīe mōten wiþ þē sprecan. Ne wiern þū him þæs! Hīe þæs wierþe þynċaþ þæt hīe hwate męnn dōmes belęcgen. Hūru hira lāttēow dēah sē-þe hīe hider lǣdde.'

129. Þā cwæþ Hrōþgār: 'Iċ cūþe hine þā hē cniht wæs. His fæder hātte Ęcgþēow. Sē hæfde tō wīfe Hrēþles dohtor, Ġēata cyninges; næfde hē dohtor būtan hīe. And nū is his nesa hider cumen: sohte holdne frēond! Þæt sæġdon þā sċipmęnn þe Ġēata sęlena hider brohton þæt hē hæbbe þrītiġra manna stręnġo on his handgripe. Iċ wēne, God self hine sęnde ūs tō fultume wiþ Gręndles brōgan; iċ him sċeal māþmas bēodan for his snelsċipe. Bēo þū on ofoste; hāt hine inn-gān mid his ġefērum! Sęġe him ēac þæt hīe ūs wilcuman sind hider ofer sǣ.'

130. Þā ġe·cierde Wulfgār eft tō þǣm ġiesthūse, and his ǣrende ā·bēad, and him tō cwæþ: 'Ēow hēt sęcgan mīn hlāford, Hrōþgār cyning, þæt hē ēowre ġebyrda cann, and ġē him wilcuman sind hider ofer sǣ. Nū ġē mōton gān on ēowrum hęreġeatwum Hrōþgār ġesēon. Lǣtaþ ēowre sċieldas and ēowru speru hēr on·bīdan þǣre sprǣce ġeęndunge.'

131. Þā ā·rās Bēowulf mid his þeġna hēape. Hira sume hē lǣfde him bæftan, and him bebēad þæt hīe þā wǣpnu hēolden. Þā ēode Bēowulf under Heorotes hrōf, þæt hē on þǣm heorþe ġestōd. Þā grētte hē Hrōþgār cyning fæġerum wordum, and him tō cwæþ:

132. 'Hāl wes þū Hrōþgār! Iċ eom Hyġelāces mǣġ and þeġn; fela mǣrliċra dǣda iċ fręmede on ġeogoþe. Mē wearþ Gręndles þing cūþ on mīnum lande. Þæt sæġdon sċipmęnn þæt þēos heall stande īdel and unnytt siþþan ǣfen cymþ, þēah hit sīe ealra hūsa bętst.

133. 'Þā ġelǣrdon mē þā witan on mīnum lande þæt iċ þē sohte; for·þǣm hīe mīne stręnġo cūþon: ġesāwon mē of wīge blōdiġne cuman, þǣr iċ eotena cynn ūte on gārsęcge for·slōg and for·dyde, and hira fīfe ġeband.

134. 'Nū wile iċ þē, Dęna cyning, ānre bēne biddan, nū iċ þus feorran cōm, þæt iċ āna mōte mid mīnra þeġna werode Heorot fǣlsian! Iċ hæbbe ēac ġehīered þæt Gręndel for his rēþnesse neręċþ nānra wǣpna. Iċ þæt þonne for·hycge—swā mē mīn hlāford, Hyġelāc cyning, bliþe sīe—þæt iċ sweord tō wīge bere oþþe sċield: mid barum handum iċ him wiþ-fō. Þæt biþ stīþ ġemōt, þonne wit tō·gædre fōþ!

135. 'Wēn is, ġif hē siġe hæfþ, þæt hē wile Ġēatas for·swelgan unforhtlīċe, swā hē ǣr Dęne dyde. Ġif iċ on wīge ā·fealle, ne þearft þū mē bebyriġan, ne ymb mīnne līchaman sorgian! Ac ġif mē wīg nimþ, on·sęnd Hyġelāce mīne byrnan; sēo is Hrēþles lāf, and Wēlandes ġeweorc, þæs mǣran smiþes. Wyrd gǣþ ā swā hēo sċeal!'

136. Þā cwæþ Hrōþgār: 'For ġefeohtum þū ūs sohtest and for fultume, mīn frēond Bēowulf! Sorg is mē tō sęcganne hwelċe iermþa mē Gręndel ġedōn hæfþ mid his hęrġunge. Mīne þeġnas sind of·slæġene, and mīn folgoþ is ġewanod.

137. 'Full·oft ġebēotodon mīne þeġnas, þā hīe druncne æt hira ġebēorsċipe sǣton, þæt hīe wolden Gręndle mid ġefeohte wiþ·standan; ac þæs on morgenne, siþþan hit dagode, wǣron þā bęnċa mid blōde begotene; þā hæfde iċ þeġna þȳ lǣs.'

138. Þā cwæþ hē eft: 'Site nū tō þǣm ġebēorsċipe, and bēo blīþe mid þīnum ġefērum, swā þē þīn mōd hwętt!'

Hū Dęne and Ġēatas wistfullodon on þǣm ġebēorsċipe.

139. Þā wæs þǣm Ġēatum bęnċ ġerȳmed on þǣre healle, þǣr hīe sittan ēodon ealle æt·samne. Þā behēold se byrele swīþe wel his note: ēode æfter bęnċum, and medo sċęnċte and hlūtor ealo. Þā on·gann se sċop singan and ġieddian beorhtre stemne. Þā męnn wǣron blīþe; þæt wæs miċel ġesamnung Dęna and Ġēata!

140. Þā wæs þǣr sum mann, Unferþ hātte, sē æt þæs cyninges fōtum sæt, for·þǣmþe hē wæs þæs cyninges þyle. And se Unferþ wæs swīþe æfestiġ mann: ne ūþe hē nā þæt ǣniġ ōþer mann māran weorþmynt hæfde þonne hē self. And for þǣm wæs him Bēowulfes sīþ miċel æfþanca.

141. Þā cwæþ Unferþ: 'Eart þū se Bēowulf sē-þe wiþ Brecan ymb sund flite, þonne ġit for ġielpe incrum fēorum nēþdon ūte on gārsęcge? Þæt wæs on wintra þæt ġit ūt on sǣ swummon. Ac nān mann, ne lēof ne lāþ, ne mihte inc þæs sīþes for·wiernan. Seofon niht ġit on ȳþum swuncon. Hē þē ofer·flāt æt sunde, for·þǣm hē māran stręngo hæfde. Þā þæs on morgenne hine sǣ on land wearp; þanon hē ġesohte his āġenne eard, Brandinga land: hē his bēot wiþ þē befullan ġelǣste. Nū wēne iċ þē wiersan ġemētinge, ġif þū dearst ofer niht bīdan on Gręndles nēawiste.'

142. Þā cwæþ Bēowulf: 'Hwæt þū, mīn frēond Unferþ, fela sprǣce ymb Brecan sīþ! Fela īdles þū spriċst! Iċ sęcge þē tō sōþe þæt iċ māran stręngo hæfde on sunde, and māran frēcennessa ġenēþde þonne hē oþþe ǣniġ ōþer mann. Næs hit nā swā þū sęġst. Ac nū sċealt þū þæt sōþ ġehīeran hū hit ymb unc Brecan ġelamp:—

143. 'Þæt is þæt wit on cnihthāde ġecwǣdon and ġebēotodon þæt wit uncrum fēorum ġenēþden ūte on gārsęcge. And wit þæt ġelǣston swā. Wit hæfdon nacod sweord on handum þā wit ūt-swummon: þohton unc wiþ þā sǣdēor węrian. Ne mihte hē mē nā oþ·swimman: iċ him fram nolde.

144. 'Wit wǣron fīf niht ūte on gārsęcge. Þā ġelamp unc yfele on þǣre fare, þæt unc on-becōm swīþe hrēoh weder, and unc sēo wōde sǣ and se stranga norþwind wīde tō·drāf.

145. 'Þā wearþ þāra sǣdēora mōd ā·hwętt. Hira ān mē ġefēng and tō grunde ġetēah; hwæþre mē Dryhten for·ġeaf þæt iċ hine mid sweorde of·stang. Þæt is miċel wundor þæt iċ āna mē ā·węrede wiþ eall þā sǣdēor! Iċ him þæs lēan for·ġeald þæt hīe mīn swā þearle ehton. Næfdon hīe þone ġefēan þæt hīe mē him tō męte þiġeden, sittende æt hira ġebēorsċipe on þǣre sǣ grunde! Ac þæs on morgenne lāgon hīe uppe, swīþe for·wundode, oþ-þæt hīe sǣ on land wearp. Swā iċ of·slōg nigon niceras.

146. 'Þā sċān sēo sunne sūþan, and þā ȳþa wurdon ġestilde. Þā wæs iċ tō þǣm wēriġ þæt iċ ne mihte furþor swimman, ac mē sǣ on land wearp.

147. 'Ne ġehīerde iċ nǣfre be þē þæt þū swā mǣrliċe dǣda ġefrę̄medest; þēah þū þīnum ġebrōþrum tō banan wurde, þæs þū sċealt on hęlle wīte drēogan, þēah þīn ġewitt duge. Iċ sęcge þē tō sōþe, Unferþ, þæt Gręndel nǣfre swā miċel yfel ne ġedyde, ġif þīn mōd swā unforht wǣre swā þū self tęlst. Ac hē hæfþ on·funden þæt hē ne þearf him þā fǣhþe on·drǣdan: ne wēnþ hē him nānes wīges tō Dęnum! Ac iċ him sċeal sōna Ġēata wīgcræft ġelǣran! Tō·morgen sċeal ēower ġehwelċ orsorg tō ġebēorsċipe gān sōna swā hit dagaþ!'

148. Þā wearþ se cyning blīþe: ġelīefde him helpe, siþþan hē ġehīerde Bēowulfes fæstrǣdne ġeþoht.

149. Þā ēode Wealhþēo forþ, sēo cwēn, and þā męnn grētte. Ǣrest hēo sealde þā cuppan Hrōþgāre cyninge, and bæd hine þæt hē blīþe wǣre æt þǣm ġebēorsċipe, and his mannum hold.

150. Þā ēode hēo æfter bęnċum, and þā cuppan eallum sealde ġe ealdum ġe ġeongum, oþ-þæt hēo tō Bēowulfe cōm, and him þā cuppan brohte, and hine grētte: þancode Gode mid snotrum wordum þæt hire se willa ġelamp þæt hēo mōste frōfre wēnan þāra iermþa þe hīe swā lange drugon.

151. Hē þā Bēowulf on·fēng þǣre cuppan æt þǣre cwēne handa. Þā wearþ his mōd on·bryrd, and hē cwæþ: 'Þā iċ on sċip ā·stāg mid mīnum ġefērum, þā þohte iċ þæt iċ āhwæþer wolde, oþþe þīnra lēoda willan ġewyrċan, oþþe on wīge feallan. Nū tō·niht iċ sċeal mīnne þeġnsċipe ġecȳþan, oþþe mīnes līfes ęnde ġebīdan.'

152. Þā ġelīcode þǣre cwēne Bēowulfes ġielpsprǣc. Hēo ēode þā tō þǣm cyninge sittan.

153. Þā wæs eft swā ǣr bliss and hleahtor on þǣre healle, oþ-þæt se cyning wolde his ręste sēċan. Þā ā·rās eall þæt werod. Þā grētte ǣġþer ōþerne, Hrōþgār Bēowulf; and se cyning cwæþ: 'Nǣfre ǣr ne be·tǣhte iċ Dęna ġemōtærn ǣnigum męnn tō healdanne būtan þē ānum. Hafa nū and ġeheald þæt æþele hūs! Ġemyne þīnra mǣrþa, and ġecȳþ þīnne þeġnsċipe! Waca wiþ fēond! Ne biþ þē nānes gōdes wana, ġif þū þē ġesund bierġst!'

Hū Bēowulf ġefeaht wiþ Gręndel.

154. Þā ġewāt Hrōþgār cyning ūt of þǣre healle; ne lǣfde hē him bæftan būtan þā Ġēatas āne.

155. Þā dyde Bēowulf his byrnan of and his helm, and hīe his handþeġne sealde and his sweord samod, þæt hē hīe ġehēolde. Þā spræc Bēowulf ġielpword ǣr hē on będd stige, þus cweþende: 'Ne tęlle iċ mē nā eargran þonne Gręndel selfne! For þǣm nyle iċ hine mid sweorde of·slēan, þēah iċ ēaþe mihte. Ne cann hē sweordes wealdan oþþe sċieldes, þēah hē cēne sīe. Wit tō·niht sċulon wǣpnu ofer·sittan, ġif hē mē wiþ·standan dearr. Dēme siþþan se ælmihtiga þone siġe on swā hwæþre hand swā him ġemet þynċþ!'

156. Þā on·hielde Bēowulf his hēafod tō þǣm bolstre, and his ġefēran swā same. Hira nān ne þohte þæt hē sċolde eft tō his earde becuman, oþþe his māgas and frīend eft ġesēon. Ac hīe wǣron sōna on fæstum slǣpe, ealle būtan Bēowulfe: sē wacode on·ġēan þæs fēondes cyme, ięrre on mōde.

157. Þā cōm se ā·wierġda Gręndel of þǣm mōrum stealcian

under þiċċum miste; þohte þāra manna sumne besierwan on Heorote.

158. Sōna swā hē tō þǣre healle cōm, swā arn hē þā duru on. Þā on·ġeat hē þæt hēo wæs fæste belocen. Þā wearþ hē ierre, and þā duru ġelæhte mid swīþliċre mihte and of heorrum ā·hōf. Hē ēode þā inn, rēþe on mōde; of his ēagum stōd leoht swelċe fȳr.

159. Þā ġeseah hē þā Ġēatas on þǣre healle slǣpan. Þā ā·hlōg his mōd: þohte þæt hē hīe for·swelgan wolde ǣnne æfter ōþrum ǣr dæġ cōme. Ac Bēowulf wacode: behēold hū se fēond faran wolde.

160. Ne ielde Grendel nā lange, ac hē hraþe ġefēng slǣpendne mann, and hine siþþan styċċemǣlum tō·bræġd: tō·bræc þā bān mid his tusċum, and þæt blōd of þǣm ǣdrum dranc, oþ-þæt hē ealne þone līchaman for·swolgen hæfde mid handum mid fōtum mid ealle.

161. Hē ēode þā furþor, and Bēowulf ġelæhte, on his bedde licgende. Þā ġesæt Bēowulf wiþ earm, and him tō·ġēanes fēng. Þā on·ġeat Grendel sōna þæt hē ne ġemētte ǣr on ǣnigum menn māran handgripe!

162. Þā wearþ hē forht on mōde: wolde flēon tō þǣm mōrum, þǣr hē his wununge wiste mid þǣm ōþrum sċuccum. Næs his drohtoþ on Heorote swelċe hē ǣr ġemētte!

163. Þā ġemunde Bēowulf þāra ġielpworda þe hē ǣr ġespræc: stōd þā ūplang, and him fæstlīċe wiþ-fēng. Þā wæs Grendel ūtweard. Ac Bēowulf him fram nolde: ġefēng hine þȳ fæstor, þēah him þā fingras ful·nēah bursten. Swā hīe mid unġemetlīċe nīþe winnende wǣron, oþ-þæt sēo heall dynede, and maniġe þāra benċa fram þǣm syllum ā·bugon. Þæt wæs miċel wundor þæt sēo heall ne ā·hrure grundlunga. Ac hēo ne fēoll nā, for·þǣmþe hēo wæs swiþe fæste mid īsenbendum besmiþod innan and ūtan. Þæt sæġdon ēac

Dęna witan þæt nān mann ne mihte þæt hūs tō·brecan būtan hit man mid fȳre for·bærnde

164. Þā tugon Bēowulfes ġefēran hira sweord þæt hīe hira hlāford węreden. Hīe þā þider urnon ealle, and þā cęmpan bēġen ymb·þrungon, and on ǣlċe healfe hēowon, Gręndles feorh sēċende. Hīe nyston þæt nān sweord ne mihte þone fēond grētan, for·þǣm hē hæfde eallum wǣpnum for·sworen mid his drȳcræfte.

165. Hē þā Gręndel, siþþan hē on·ġeat þæt hē þanon æt·berstan ne mihte, þā hrīemde hē ęġeslīċe, swā þæt ealle Dęne hit ġehīerdon, ġe furþum þā weardas on þǣm wealle ā·fyrhte wǣron.

166. Þā wearþ wund ġesīenu on Gręndles eaxle, oþ-þæt þā sina on·sprungon and þā bān tō·burston. Hē þā æt·bærst þanon, tō dēaþe ġewundod: flēah tō þǣm mōrum, þæt hē him on his fæstenne burge. Hē ġefrēdde þēah þæt his līf wæs æt ęnde.

167. Swā Bēowulf ġelǣste his ġielp: fǣlsode þæs cyninges healle, and Dęnum þā yfel ġebētte þe hīe lange drugon. Þæt wæs sweotol tācen þā Bēowulf ġenam Gręndles earm and eaxle, and hīe on þǣm stapole ā·sętte æt þǣre healle dura, eallum mannum tō wǣfersīene.

168. Þæs on morgenne wæs þǣr miċel męniġo ymb þā healle, ġe ealde ġe ġeonge. Þæs cyninges ealdormęnn cōmon feorran and nēan þæt hīe þæt wundor ġesāwen. Gręndles dēaþ ne þuhte hira ǣnigum sārliċ.

169. Hīe þā Gręndle æfter-spyredon oþ hīe tō męre cōmon, 'nicera męre' hātte, þǣr Gręndel his fæsten hæfde. Þā ġesāwon hīe þæt þæt wæter wæs eall mid blōde ġedrēfed.

170. Hīe þā him hāmweard węndon of þǣm męre, ealde witan and ġeonge hagostealdmęnn ealle æt·gædere, on swiftum horsum rīdende.

171. On þǣm weġe hīe sprǣcon fela ymb Bēowulf. Hīe cwǣdon þæt nān bętera cęmpa nǣre norþ ne sūþ ġeond ealle eorþan, ne rīċes wierþra. Ne tǣldon hīe hūru hira āgenne hlāford, ac cwǣdon þæt hē wǣre gōd cyning.

172. Hwilum hīe on ġeflite ærndon, þǣr him þā wegas fæġere þuhton.

173. Þā wæs þǣr mid him sum cyninges þeġn, sē wæs gōd sċop. Hē on·gann þā Bēowulfes sīþ on lēoþwīsan ā·sęcgan mid wel-ġesęttum wordum. Þā on·gann hē cweþan be Siġemunde þǣm mǣran wręċċan and Fitelan, hū hīe bēġen æt·gædere, ēam and nefa, fela mǣrliċra dǣda ġefręmedon. Þā cwæþ hē þæt sēo dǣd þe ealra mǣrlicost wæs, þæt hē þā ġefręmede him āna—næs him Fitela mid.

174. Þæt wæs þā hē þone dracan on his sċræfe ā·cwealde, þā hē under þone hāran stān ġenēþde, and hine hętelīċe þiede, þæt þæt sweord on þæs sċræfes wealle æt·stōd. Þā sōna ġemealt se draca, fram his āgenre hǣtan for·swǣled. Siġemund hæfde þā mīd his snelsċipe þæs dracan goldhord ġegān. Hē þā þæt gold and þā māþmas ealle on his sċip bær, and wearþ swā wręċċena mǣrost.

175. Þā sæġdon hīe ealle þæt Siġemund næfde ġefręmed mǣrliċran dǣda þonne Bēowulf. Swā hīe forþ ēodon, blīþe on mōde, oþ-þæt hīe tō Heorote cōmon.

176. Þā wæs se cyning ēac þider cumen, mōdiġlīċe stæppende on·middan his þeġna hēape, and sēo cwēn samod mid hire mæġdena hēape. Þā-þā Hrōþgār tō þǣre healle cōm, and on þǣm stapole ġestōd, and Gręndles hand ġeseah, þā cwæþ hē:

177. 'Sīe Dryhtne þanc þisse ansīene! Iċ hæbbe fela bismra ġebiden æt Gręndles handum. Næs þæt ġēara þæt iċ nānre bōte ne wēnde þāra iermþa þe wē lange drugon. Ne wēndon ēac mīne witan þæt hīe mihten Dęna lēode wiþ þā sċuccan be·węrian. Ac God mæġ ā wyrċan wundor æfter wundre! And nū hæfþ feorrancund mann dǣd ġefręmed þe wē ǣr ne mihton þurh·tēon mid ūre ealra snytro! Hwæt, þæt wīf þe swelċne sunu ġebær, ġif hēo ġīet leofaþ, hēo mæġ sęcgan þæt hire God ēstiġ wǣre on hire bearntēame!

178. 'Lēofa Bēowulf, nū þū eart þeġna bętst, iċ wile þē swelċe sunu lufian; heald wel forþ þā nīwan sibbe! Ne biþ þē nānes gōdes wana þæs-þe iċ ġeweald hæbbe. Oft iċ lēanode lǣssan dǣda wācran þeġne! þū hæfst mid þīnum dǣdum ġefręmed þæt þīn dōm leofaþ ā būtan ęnde.'

179. þā andswarode Bēowulf: 'Wē þæt ġeswinc and þæt ġewinn blīþeliċe drēogende wǣron. Ac mē lēofre wǣre þæt þū hine selfne ġesēon mōste! Iċ þohte hine fæste ġebindan; ac God ne ūþe mē þæt iċ him flēames for·wiernde, þēah iċ him ġeorne æt·fulge: hē wæs mē tō strang on fēþe. Hē for·lēt þēah his earm him behindan. Ne þearf hē him lęnġran līfes wēnan, þēah hē æt·burste: is sēo wund tō dēop. Hē sċeal þæs miċlan dōmes on·bīdan, hū him se ælmihtiga wile dēman.'

180. þa ġeswīgode Unferþ his ġielpsprǣce, þā hē Gręndles hand ġeseah and þā fingras: wǣron þā næġlas swā hearde swā stīele and swā sċearpe. Ealle sæġdon þæt nān wǣpen ne mihte hine grētan, ne þā hand for·ċeorfan.

181. þā hēt man Heorot innan frætwian. þǣr wǣron maniġe weras and maniġ wīf þe þā healle ġearcodon, and þā wāgas mid dēorwierþum godewębbe bewrigon.

182. Ac þæt æþele hūs wæs swīþe tō·brocen innanweard ofer eall, and þā heorras tō·hlidene. Se hrōf āna þurh·wunode ansund.

183. þā ēode se cyning tō þǣre healle, and sæt mid his mannum blissiġende samod. Næs nǣfre ǣr swā miċel þeġna hēap ymb hira cyning; and nǣfre þeġnas bęt ġebǣrdon!

184. Þā for·ġeaf se cyning Bēowulfe gyldenne seġn, his siġes tō lēane, swelċe ēac helm, and byrnan, and dēorwierþe sweord. Ne þorfte Bēowulf nā sċamian þāra ġiefena! Þā hēt se cyning lǣdan inn eahta hors; þāra ān hæfde sadol on: þæt wæs þæs cyninges wīghors. Þā for·ġeaf hē Bēowulfe þā hors tō·ēacan þǣm ōþrum māþmum: hēt hine þāra wel brūcan. Swā manlīċe lēanode him se gōda cyning his þeġnsċipe!

185. Þā·ġiet se cyning sealde Bēowulfes ġefērum dēorwierþe māþmas; and hēt þone ānne mid fēo for·ġieldan þe Grendel ǣr ā·cwealde.

186. Þā mihte man ġehīeran eft swā ǣr þǣre hearpan swēġ. Þā on·gann þæs cyninges sċop lēoþ singan be Hengeste and Finne, hū Finn on his āgenre byriġ of·slæġen wearþ.

187. Þā þæt lēoþ ā·sungen wæs, þā wæs eft swā ǣr hleahtor and gamen on Heorote, and þā byrelas sċencton wīn of gyldenum fatum.

188. Þā cōm Wealhþēo forþ, mid gyldenre cynewiþþan ġefrætwod: ēode þǣr Hrōþgār and Hrōþwulf æt·gædere sǣton, ēam and nefa. Þā cwæþ hēo: 'On·fō þisse cuppan, mīn hlāford, Hrōþgār cyning! Bēo blīþe, and tō Ġēatum sprec mildum wordum, and lēana him mid ġiefum, swā cyninge ġedafenaþ! Þū hæfst nū gōdne friþ, feorran and nēan: Heorot is ġefǣlsod.

189. 'Brūc þīnes cynerīċes swā lange swā þū mōte, and hit þīnum māgum lǣf, þonne þū ġewītan sċealt! Iċ cann mīnne glædne Hrōþwulf þæt hē wile uncru ġemǣnu bearn ārlīċe healdan, ġif þū ǣr ġewītst þonne hē. Iċ wēne þæt hē wile uncrum bearnum mid gōde lēanian eall þæt wit him tō willan and tō āre ġedydon, ġif hē þæt ġeman.'

190. Þā ēode hēo þǣr hire suna twēġen sǣton, Hrēþrīċ and Hrēþmund, and maniġe æþelinga suna mid him. Þǣr sæt ēac Bēowulf be þǣm twǣm ġebrōþrum. Þā bær hēo him þā cuppan, and him hræġl īewde and miċelne healsbēag, and hine grētte mildum wordum, and spræc þus beforan eallum þǣm werode:

191. 'Brūc þisses hræġles and þisses bēages, lēofa Bēowulf, and ġeþēoh wel! Bēo þissum cnihtum līþe lārēow; iċ þē þæs lēan ġeman! Hæfst þū swā ġebǣred þæt þīn lof biþ ā·rǣred ā būtan ende feorran and nēan.

192. 'Blissa nū on þǣm ġebēorsċipe! Hēr is ǣġhwelċ mann ōþrum ġetrīewe, and his hlāforde hold. Ealle sind ġeþwǣre; lustlīċe hīe dōþ swā iċ bidde.'

193. Þā sēo cwēn hire sprǣce geendode, þā ēode hēo tō þǣm cyninge sittan.

Be Grendles mēder.

194. On þisse blisse þurh·wunodon hīe oþ-þæt niht cōm. Þā ġewāt se cyning tō his būre þæt hē hine þǣr·inne ġereste. His þeġnas hē lǣfde þǣr bæftan, þæt hīe þā healle hēolden, swā hīe oft ǣr dydon.

195. Þā wearþ sēo heall mid beddum and mid bolstrum ġeond·brǣdd, and ǣlċ mann his reste sohte. Hīe setton hira sċieldas him tō hēafdum. Þǣr mihte man ġesēon ǣlċes mannes wǣpnu him ġehende licgan; for·þǣm hira þēaw wæs þæt hīe ealneweġ tō wīge ġearwe wǣron ġe æt hām ġe ūte, swā oft swā hira hlāforde þearf wæs: þæt wæs gōd folc!

196. Hīe þā sōna on·slēpon. Hira sum on·geald swīþe sārlīċe þǣre nihtreste, swā Denum oft ǣr ġelamp þurh Grendles nīþ. Nū wearþ eallum mannum cūþ þæt wrecend þā·ġīet leofode: þæt wæs Grendles mōdor. Sēo cōm on þǣre ilcan nihte tō Heorote. Þā wearþ Dena ġefēa tō ġedrēfednesse ġeċierred, siþþan Grendles mōdor inne-fealh. Ac se eġe wæs lǣssa, for·þǣmþe hit wīf wæs, næs wer.

197. Þā wearþ maniġ sweord ġetogen ġeond þā healle, and maniġ sċield ā·hafen; hīe ne ġemundon nā helm ne byrnan þā him se brōga on-becōm. Hēo wearþ þā swīþe ā·fyrht, siþþan hēo on·funden wæs: wolde ūt þanon, þæt hēo hire fēore burge. Ac hēo ġefēng hraþe þāra þeġna ānne, Æsċhęre hātte, and hine fęrede tō hire mōrfæstenne; and se Æsċhęre wæs þǣm cyninge ealra manna lēofost. Næs Bēowulf þǣr, ac him wæs ōþer būr ǣr ġeteohhod. Hēo ġenam ēac hire suna hand and eaxle, þǣr hēo hīe hangian ġeseah.

198. Þā wæs se cyning swīþe ġedrēfed on mōde, þā hē ġehīerde þæt his ġelufoda þeġn dēad wæs. Hraþe wearþ Bēowulf fetod tō þæs cyninges būre. Hē þā Bēowulf ēode sōna mid his ġefērum þǣr se cyning his bād. Þā grētte hē þone cyning, and āsċode hine ġif sēo niht him ġetǣse wǣre. Þā andswarode se cyning:

199. 'Ne āsċa þū æfter ġesǣlþum! Sorg is ġenīwod mē and mīnum folce. Æsċhęre is dēad, Eormenrīċes ieldra brōþor, mīn wita and mīn ġefēra on wīge: oft wit on ġefeohte stōdon æt·samne, uncru hēafdu węriende, þonne fēþan hniton and helmas cnysedon. Nis nān swā gōd þeġn swā hē!

200. 'Nū is him tō banan ġeworden sum unfǣlu wiht. Ne wāt iċ hwider hēo oþ·flēah mid þǣre hęrehȳþe. Hēo wræc þā fǣhþe þe þū Gręndel ā·cwealdest ġiestran-niht. Hē æt wīge ā·fēoll, and nū cōm ōþer fēond, hire sunu tō wrecanne.

201. 'Iċ þæt ġehīerde ūplęndisċe męnn sęcgan þæt hīe ġesāwen swelċe twā wihta hwearfian ġeond þā mōras. Þāra ōþer wæs, þæs-þe him þuhte, wīfe anliċ. Ōþer hæfde weres wæstm; būtan hē wæs māra þonne ǣniġ ōþer mann; þone man nęmnde Gręndel on ealddagum. Nyston hīe hwæþer hē fæder hæfde, oþþe hwæt his cynn wǣre.

202. 'Hīe eardiaþ on wēstum lande and on ǣmęnnum: nabbaþ him tō ġefērum būtan wulfas and wildēor. Nis þæt land manigum ġefēre, for·þǣm þǣr sind sċearpe wegas and stānihte, and hēa clifu, and wilde mōras. And þǣr is miċel męre on·middan þǣm mōrum, þe man hǣtt "nicera męre." And of þǣm męre ān ēa is iernende mid unġefōglicum strēame, hwīlum bufan eorþan, hwīlum under eorþan, oþ-þæt hēo ūt-sċīett on gārsęcg.

203. 'Nis hit feorr heonon þæt se męre stęnt under hārum stāne. Of þǣm stāne sind ā·weaxene swiþe hrīmiġe bearwas, þe þæt wæter ofer·helmiaþ; and þæt wæter is sweart under þǣm clife neoþan. Þǣr man mæġ miċel wundor on niht ġesēon, swelċe eall þæt wæter biernende wǣre. Nān swā wīs mann ne leofaþ þæt hē þone grund wite.

204. 'Nān mann þǣr eardian ne mæġ; ac for þǣm maniġfealdum brōgum and ęġesum and for þǣre ānnesse þæs wīdġillan wēstennes hit nǣniġ mann ā·drēogan ne mæġ, ac hit ǣlċ mann for þǣm beflīehþ, ġe furþum wildēor. Ġif hit ġelimpþ þæt heorot þone wudu sēċe for hunda ęġe, him biþ lēofre þæt hē his līf þǣr on ōfre for·lǣte þonne hē inn wile on þæt wæter. Þæt is unhīeru stōw: is þæt wæter sweart, and mid stormum hrēoh; ǣfre hit riġnþ þǣr, swelċe heofon wēope.

205. 'Nū is eft swā ǣr rǣd æt þē ānum ġelang! Ne canst þū ġīet þā frēcnan stōwe þǣr þū hīe findan miht; sēċ, ġif þū dyrre! Iċ þē þā fǣhþe mid fēo lēaniġe and mid dēorwierþum māþmum, swā iċ ǣr dyde, ġif þū on·weġ-cymst.'

206. Þā cwæþ Bēowulf: 'Ne sorga þū, snotra mann! Bętere is ǣġhwelċum þæt hē his frēond wrece þonne hē fela murne. Ūre ǣġhwelċ sċeal ġebīdan his līfes ęnde. Ġewyrċe, sē-þe mōte, dōm ǣr his dēaþe! þæt biþ him bętst æfter his dæġe. Ā·rīs, Hrōþgār cyning! Uton hraþe faran! Uton Grendles mēder æfter-spyrian! Iċ hit þē ġehāte: ne losaþ hēo nā, ne on lande ne on sǣ, ne on sǣs grunde, gā þǣr hēo wile! Þȳs dæġe hafa ġeþyld þīnra iermþa, swā iċ þē wēne tō!'

207. Þā ā·hlēop se ealda cyning, Dryhtne þanciende þæs-þe Bēowulf ġespræc. Þā ġewāt hē þanon, on horse rīdende, and maniġe his þeġna mid him. Þā lāstas wǣron ieþġesīene, þǣr Grendles mōdor þæs þeġnes līchaman ferede. Hīe drifon þæt spor ġeond æceras and mǣdwa ūt of þǣm bȳnan lande inn on þone weald, siþþan ūt on þone mōr.

208. Þā ēodon hīe tō þǣm stānihtan lande, þǣr þā paþas sticole wǣron and swīþe nearwe. Þā ēode se cyning beforan, fēowera sum his witena, for·þǣm hē cūþe bętst þone weġ. Þā fǣringa hīe ġesāwon þā for·sēarodan bēamas ofer þone hāran stān hangian and þone sweartan męre under·neoþan.

209. Þā wearþ þǣm cyninge and his witum swīþe ange on mōde, þā hīe Æsċhęres hēafod on þǣm ōfre ġemētton, and ġesāwon hū þæt wæter wæs eall mid blōde ġedrēfed. Þā blēow man horn, and ġesamnode þæt werod. Hīe þā ealle wīcodon be þǣm męre. Hīe ġesāwon maniġra cynna nǣdran and sǣdracan on þǣm wætere swimman, swelċe ēac niceras on þǣm næssum licgan. Hīe þā ealle ierre on·weġ-hruron, sōna swā hīe þone horn ġehīerdon. Þāra ānne Bēowulf mid flāne of·sċēat: ġelętte hine his sundes. Þā wearþ hē mid sperum tō·sticod and mid hōcum on land ġetogen; þā męnn sċēawodon þone ęġeslican ġiest.

Hū Bēowulf of·slōg Grendles mōdor.

210. Þā ġierede hine Bēowulf mid his hęreġeatwum: dyde on his byrnan, and sętte him helm on hēafod. Þone helm worhte sum cræftiġ smiþ on ealddagum; sē hine mid eofera anlīcnessum besętte, þæt hine nān sweord bītan ne mihte.

Bēowulf hæfde ēac swīþe ǣnliċ sweord; þæs him on·lāh Unferþ, þæs cyninges þyle, þā him wæs gōdes wǣpnes þearf. Þæt wæs eald lāf: ne swāc hit nǣfre æt wīge. Hūru ne ġemunde Unferþ his ǣrran ġielpes, þā hē Bēowulfe þæs sweordes on·lāh: ne dorste his fēore ġenēþan under þǣm hrēom ȳþum. Þǣr ā·læġ his dōm, þæt hē þā æt nīehstan hine selfne tō nahte bemæt. Næs hit Bēowulfe swā, siþþan hē hine tō wīge ġeġiered hæfde. Þā cwæþ Bēowulf:

211. 'Ġeþęnċ nū, þū snotra cyning, nū iċ eom fūs tō sīþianne, hwæt wit ǣr ġesprǣcon: ġif iċ æt þīnre þearfe mīn līf for·lēte, þæt þū mē ā wǣre on fæder stǣle æfter mīnum forþsīþe. Bēo þū mundbora mīnum þeġnum, ġif iċ on wīge ā·fealle! On·sęnd ēac, lēofa Hrōþgār, Hyġelāce þā māþmas þe þū mē ǣr sealdest, þæt hē mæġe on·ġietan, þonne hē on þæt gold staraþ, þæt iċ cystiġne mundboran funde. And lǣt Unferþ mīn dēorwierþe sweord habban; iċ wile mē mid Hruntinge dōm ġewyrċan, oþþe mē sċeal dēaþ niman.'

212. Þā efste Bēowulf unforhtlīċe æfter þissum wordum: hē nolde nānre andsware bīdan, ac þǣr·rihte intō þǣm męre sċēat, and under þā ȳþa dēaf. Sęgþ þæt spell þæt hē ealne dæġ niþer swamm ǣr hē mihte þone grund on·ġietan.

213. Þā under þǣm on·funde Gręndles mōdor þæt sum mann sċuccena eardes ufan fandode. Grāp þā him tō·ġēanes, and hine ġefēng mid hire ęġeslicum clāwum. Ac hēo ne mihte him naht lāþes ġedōn: ne mihte hēo nā þā īsenan hringas mid hire fingrum þurh·fōn. Ac hēo hine fæste befēng, þæt hē ne mihte his sweordes wealdan, ne hine wiþ þā sǣdēor węrian, þe hine on þǣm sunde swīþe swęnċton mid hira tusċum.

214. Þā on·ġeat Bēowulf þæt hē on sumre healle wæs, þǣr him þæs wæteres flōd naht dęrian ne mihte for þǣm hrōfe. Þæt is ēac miċel wundor þæt hē leoht ġeseah inne on þǣre healle beorhte sċīnende.

215. Þā on·ġeat hē þæt mihtiġe męrewīf, and þā rǣsde on hīe, and hīe on þæt hēafod slōg, þæt hit hlēoþrode mid þǣm dynte, swelċe þæt sweord sum ęġeslic wīglēoþ sunge. Þā on·ġeat hē þæt þæt sweord nolde bītan; ac him sēo ęcg ġeswāc æt þǣre þearfe, þēah hit oft ǣr on wīge dohte. Þæt wæs se forma sīþ þæt þǣm sweorde his dōm ā·læġ.

216. Þā wearþ Bēowulf ānrǣd swā ǣr, and his mǣrþa ġemunde. Hē wearp þā þæt sweord of·dūne, ierre on mōde, þæt hit on eorþan læġ; and his mæġne ġetrīewde, swā þeġn sċeal dōn, ġif hē him wile langsum word æt his ęnde ġewyrċan, and ne caraþ ymb his līf. Ne rohte hē þǣre fǣhþe: ġefēng þæt wīf be hire feaxe, and hīe on eorþan wearp. Ac hēo him þæt grimme for·ġeald, þā hēo hine ġefēng and ofer·wearp, þæt hē on fielle wearþ, and hire seax ġetēah: wolde hire sunu wrecan.

217. Hē hæfde þā for·sīþod, būtan hine sēo byrne ġesċilde, and him þæs God ūþe þæt hē eft ā·stōd. Þā ġeseah hē sweord on þǣm wāge hangian. Þæt wæs eald lāf, ealra wǣpna bętst. Hit wæs māre þonne ǣniġ ōþer mann a·hębban mihte. Hē þā þæt sweord ġefēng, līfes orwēna, and hit of sċēaþe ā·tēah, and þæt wīf hętelīċe slōg on þone heals, þæt sēo ęcg eall þurh·wōd ġe flǣsċ ġe bānhringas. Hēo þā mid þǣm dynte niþer ā·sāg, and hire līf ā·lēt.

218. Þā ġefeah Bēowulf þæs weorces miċlum ġefēan; ac hē wæs wilniende þæt hē þæs ġewinnes mihte māre ġefręmman: wolde Gręndle for·ġieldan þā unārīmedlican hęrġunga þe hē on Dęnum ǣr ġeworhte. Hē þā funde hine on his ręste dēadne licgan: ne wearþ sēo wund ġehǣled þe hē ǣr on Heorote on·fēng. Þā ċearf hē him þæt hēafod of mid ānum dynte, þæt þæt bodiġ wīde sprang, and þæt hēafod forþ wand on þā flōre.

Hū Bēowulf brohte þǣm cyninge Grendles hēafod.

219. Sōna þæt ġesāwon þā witan þe mid Hrōþgāre þone męre hēoldon þæt þæt wæter wæs eall mid blōde ġedrēfed. Þā on·gunnon hīe ymb Bēowulf tō sprecanne: cwǣdon þæt hīe ne wēndon þæt hē ǣfre eft cōme Hrōþgār sēċan, for·þǣm hīe ealle untwēogendlīċe wēndon þæt hine þæt męrewīf of·slæġen hæfde.

220. Þā cōm nōn; þā for·lēton hīe þone męre, and him hāmweard węndon. Ac þā Ġēatas belifon þǣr bæftan: sǣton him on þǣm ōfre sēoce on mōde, and on þone męre starodon. Hīe wȳsċton, and þēah ne wēndon, þæt hīe hira hlāford eft ġesāwen.

221. Þā under þǣm on·gann þāra ęnta sweord wanian swelċe hit īses ġiecel wǣre; wæs Grendles blōd tō þǣm hāt and ǣtren. Wæs þæt miċel wundor þæt hit eall ġemealt būtan þǣm hilte ānum! Þā nam Bēowulf þæt hilt and Grendles hēafod samod, and nān þing ęlles, þēah hē þǣr maniġe māþmas ġeseah.

222. Þā ēode hē ūt of Grendles healle, and wearþ hraþe on sunde: dēaf ūp þurh þæt wæter. Ne ehton his nā þā sǣdēor, swā hīe ǣr dydon, for·þǣm se męre wæs eall ġefǣlsod siþþan Grendel dēad wæs.

223. Hē cōm þā tō lande swimman, swiþe ġefēonde þǣre byrþenne þe hē him mid hæfde. Þā ēodon his þeġnas him tō·ġēanes, Gode þanciende þæt hīe hine mōsten ġesundne ġesēon, and him of-dydon helm and byrnan; of þǣm drēap wæter wiþ blōd ġemęnġed.

224. Hīe þā fōron þanon, bliþe on mōde. Hira fēowere earfoþlīċe þæt hēafod fęredon on stęnġe. Ēodon swā forþ be þǣm cūþum wegum oþ-þæt hīe tō Heorote cōmon. Þā cōm Bēowulf inn-gān on þā healle, and grētte þone cyning.

Þā wearþ Gręndles hēafod be feaxe inn-boren and þǣre mōdor samod, þǣm mannum tō wǣfersīene. Ealle wundrodon þǣre seldcūþan ġesihþe.

225. Þā cwæþ Bēowulf: 'Hwæt, wē þē þās sǣlāc hider brohton, Hrōþgār cyning, þæs siġes tō tācne! Iċ hīe under wætere earfoþlīċe ġeēode. Þæt wæs heard ġefeoht: iċ þǣr for·wurde on þæs męres grunde, būtan mē God ġesċilde.'

226. Hē sæġde þā þǣm cyninge hū hine hæfde ġeworden wiþ Gręndles mōdor. Þā cwæþ hē eft: 'Iċ hit þē ġehāte þæt þū mōst on Heorote būtan sorge slǣpan, þū and þīne þeġnas: ne þearft þū þē nānne hearm on·drǣdan on þā healfe, swā þū ǣr dydest.'

227. Þā wearþ þæt gyldene hilt þǣm cyninge on hand ā·ġiefen. Hē þā se cyning sċēawode þæt hilt; on þǣm wæs ęnta ġewinn swīþe fæġere ġemearcod, swelċe hit ā·tīefred wǣre, hū hīe wiþ God wunnon, and hū hē him þæs lēan for·ġeald, þā hē hīe mid wæterflōde for·dyde. Þæt wæs þæt ǣreste ġewinn þe on þissum middanġearde ġewearþ. Þǣr wæs ēac on þǣm hilte mid rūnstafum ġemearcod and ġesętt hwǣm þæt sweord ǣrest ġeworht wǣre.

228. Þā cwæþ se cyning (ealle swīgodon): 'Þæt lā mæġ wita sęcgan, sē-þe eall ġeman þæs-þe on ealddagum ġewearþ, þæt nān swā gōd þeġn swā þū eart ne wearþ nǣfre ġeboren, mīn frēond Bēowulf! Is þīn lof ā·rǣred wīde ġeond eorþan. Ne eart þū tō swīþe ūp-āhafen for þīnum mæġne, ac þū hit mid ġeþyldum hieltst. Þū sċealt þīnum folce tō frōfre weorþan tō langre tīde.

229. 'Ne wearþ Dęnum swā Hęremōd cyning. Ne ġewēox hē him tō frōfre, ac tō forwyrde, mid·þǣmþe hē his āgne māgas slōg and ā·mierde, oþ-þæt hē of his rīċe ā·flīemed wearþ, and his līf on wræcsīþe geęndode, hwearfiende āna.

And þēah se ælmihtiga hine mid mæġne ġegōdode and mid snelsċipe ofer ealle męnn. Þā grēow hwæþre wælhrēownes on his mōde, and ġītsung, and ealle uncysta. Lǣr þē be þǣm! Iċ hæbbe þē þis bīspell ā·reaht þæt þū mæġe wīsdōm leornian.

230. 'Is miċel wundor tō sęcganne hū se ælmihtiga his ġiefa sęlþ þǣm-þe hē wile: sumum męnn hē for·ġiefþ wīsdōm, sumum þeġnsċipe. Hwīlum hē þǣm męnn his willan tō-forlǣtt tō langre tīde: sęlþ him ealle eorþan wynna, and ġedēþ him brād rīċu under·þīedd, þæt hē ne mæġ for his unwīsdōme his ęnde ġeþęnċan. Hē leofaþ on wistum. Ne ġeswęnċþ hine ādl ne sorg. Ne dręċþ hine unfriþhęre on ǣniġe healfe. Ac eall woruld him on willan węnt.

231. 'Ne cann hē þæt wierse; oþ-þæt him on·innan ofermētto weaxaþ, þonne se ęnġel slǣpþ þe þǣre sāwle ġiemþ. Is se slǣp tō fæst, and se bana nēah, sē-þe mid his bogan fācenlīċe sċīett. Þonne wierþ hē on heortan of·sċoten mid biterre flāne. Ne mæġ hē hine ġesċildan wiþ þone ā·wierġdan sċuccan; ac hē him on hand gǣþ, and wierþ his bebodum under·þīedd, and on eallum þingum færþ be his rǣde.

232. 'Þonne þynċþ him se wela tō lȳtel þe hē ǣr brūcende wæs mid unġemete. Þonne wierþ hē tō ġītsere: hordaþ his gold, and ne sęlþ hit nā his mannum, swā cyninge ġedafenaþ. Ac for þǣm hwīlwęndlicum spēdum þe him God sealde hē for·ġiett and for·ġīemþ þæt tōwearde līf.

233. 'Þonne fǣrlīċe becymþ se ęnde: se fǣġa līchama fielþ. Þonne fēhþ ōþer tō, sē-þe þā māþmas dǣlþ unhnēaw-līċe þe se ōþer hordode: ne ġīemþ nā his ęġes.

234. 'For·būg þā uncyste, lēofa Bēowulf, manna bętsta! Ġeċēos þē ēċne rǣd! Ne ġīem þū ofermētta! Nū is þīnre ġeogoþe blǣd tō lȳtelre hwīle; sōna hit biþ þæt þē ādl oþþe ieldo þīnes mæġnes benimþ, oþþe wǣpnes ęcg, oþþe fȳres fęnġ, oþþe flōdes wielm, oþþe ēagena bearhtm: ne miht þū dēaþ for·flēon!

235. 'Swā iċ Dęna rīċe hēold fīftiġ wintra, and hīe wiþ hira fīend heardlīċe bewęrede, þæt iċ nānne wiþerwinnan findan ne mihte ġeond ealne middanġeard. Hwæt mē þæs edwęnden cōm, siþþan mē Grędel wearþ onsǣġe! Gode ælmihtigum sīe þanc þæt iċ mōste starian on þæs fēondes hēafod unlibbendes, æfter uncrum ealdum ġewinne! Gā nū tō setle, and þæs ġebēorsċipes brūc! Ġefeoh þīnra mǣrþa! Þū sċealt fela māþma on·fōn, siþþan morgen biþ.'

236. Hē þā Bēowulf blissode miċlum þǣre sprǣce, and wistfullode on þǣm ġebēorsċipe, swā him se cyning bebēad. Þā wæs eft swā ǣr fæġeru ġereordung.

237. Þā cōm niht; þæt werod eall ā·rās, and se cyning his ręste sohte. Bēowulfe wæs ēac slǣpes miċel lust. Hine þā swā mēþiġne se sęleþeġn tō þǣm būre ġelǣdde þe him ǣr ġeteohhod wæs; and hē þǣr·inne slēp oþ-þæt þā fuglas mid hira sange þæt dæġred bododon.

Hū Ġēatas eft hira eard ġesohton.

238. Þā ā·rison þā Ġēatas ealle: hīe tō sċipe woldon, þæt hīe eft hira eard ġesohten.

239. Þā hēt Bēowulf Unferþe his sweord eft ā·ġiefan: hēt hine þæt sweord niman, and sæġde him þǣre lǣne þanc. Hē hęrede ēac þæt sweord: cwæþ þæt hit gōd wǣpen wǣre. On þǣm ġecȳþde Bēowulf his þeġnsċipe and his mōd þæt hē þæt sweord ne leahtrode, þēah hit him ǣr æt wīge ġeswice.

240. Þā þā Ġēatas ealle ġearwe wǣron, þā ēodon hīe þǣr Hrōþgār sæt on his cynesetle. Þā grētte Bēowulf þone cyning, and cwæþ: 'Nū wē cuman willaþ sęcgan þæt wē fūse sind Hyġelāc cyning tō sēċanne. Wē wǣron hēr on eallum þingum wel bewęnede: þū ūs wel dohtest. Ġif iċ þē tō willan māre dōn mæġ, iċ bēo sōna ġearo. Ġif iċ ġehīere ofer sǣ þæt þā nēahþēoda wiþ þē ġewinn ūp-āhębben, iċ bringe þē þūsend cęmpena tō helpe. Iċ wāt on Hyġelāce cyninge, þēah hē ġeong sīe, þæt hē mē fręmman wile mid wordum and mid weorcum, ġif þē biþ manna þearf. Ġif þonne þīn sunu, Hrēþrīċ æþeling, tō Ġēata lande þęnċþ, hē mæġ þǣr fela frēonda findan: gōd biþ þǣm þe dēah þæt hē fierlenu land sēċe.'

241. Þā andswarode him Hrōþgār: 'Se ælmihtiga þurh his wīsdōm sęnde þē þās word on mōde: ne ġehīerde iċ nǣfre swā ġeongne mann snotorlicor sprecan! Þū eart on līchaman strang, and on mōde wīs. Iċ wēne, ġif hit ġelimpþ þæt Hyġelāc on wīge ā·fielþ, oþþe him ęlles-hwæt ġesǣlþ, and þū līfes bist, þæt Ġēatas nānne bęteran cyning tō ċēosanne næbben, ġif þū þæs rīċes on·fōn wilt. Mē þīn mōd līcaþ swā lęnġ swā bęt, lēofa Bēowulf! Hæfst þū swā ġebǣred þæt sibb sċeal bēon ġemǣne þǣm folcum bǣm, Ġēatum and Dęnum, and þā ġewinn ręstan þe hīe ǣr drugon. Hūru man sċeal friþ healdan and mid ġiefum fæstnian swā lange swā iċ rīċe hæbbe. Iċ wāt þæt þā folc bā ealles fæstmōd sind ġe wiþ fēond ġe wiþ frēond on þā ealdan wīsan.'

242. Þā sealde him se cyning twelf māþmas: bæd hine mid þǣm ġiefum his āgene lēode sēċan, and hrædlīċe eft cuman. Þā cyste hine se cyning and be healse nam. Tēaras him of þǣm ēagum fēollon: wæs him se mann tō þǣm lēof þæt hē ne mihte þā tēaras for·beran. Wearþ him þæt blōd mid langoþe on·ǣled. Hē wȳsċte and wilnode þæt hē mōste hine eft ġesēon; and þēah hine þæs twēode, for·þǣm hē wæs swīþe eald.

243. Þā ġewāt Bēowulf þanon mid māþmum ġeweorþod:

ēode þǣr his þæt sċip bād. On þǣm weġe hęredon þā Ġēatas þæs cyninges cystiġnesse: þæt wæs cyning ealles orleahtre, oþ-þæt hine ieldo his mæġnes benam, swā hēo maniġe dēþ.

244. Þā Ġēatas ēodon swā forþ, oþ-þæt hīe tō þǣre sǣ strande cōmon. Þā rād him se weard tō·ġēanes. Ne grētte hē hīe nā mid hearme, swā hē ǣr dyde; ac hē him frēondlīċe tō-cwæþ: bæd hīe ġesunde tō hira sċipe gān, þǣr hit on ancre rād, mid hęreġeatwum ġehladen and mid missenlicum māþmum. Þā sealde Bēowulf þǣm bātwearde golde-fǣted sweord, þæt hē siþþan þȳ wierþra wæs for þǣm māþme, þonne hē on healle sæt.

245. Swā Bēowulf and his ġefēran of Dęna lande fōron, and tō hira āgnum lande becōmon. Sōna swā hīe tō lande cōmon, þā ēodon hīe Hyġelāc cyning grētan. And se cyning hira ġefæġen wæs, for·þǣm hē ne wēnde nā þæt hē sċolde Bēowulf his mǣġ eft libbendne ġesēon.

246. Þā on·gann se cyning hine ġeorne befriġnan hū him on þǣm sīþe ġelamp. And Bēowulf him þæt eall sweotollīċe sæġde. And þā hē his sprǣce ġeęndod hæfde, þā sealde hē þǣm cyninge þā bętstan þāra māþma þe hē him mid brohte; and hē sealde sume þā māþmas þǣre cwēne, sume his frēondum and māgum. And hīe ealle þāra ġiefena fæġnodon.

247. And se cyning weorþode Bēowulf miċlum ġe mid fēo ġe mid landāre. And Bēowulf þurh·wunode siþþan on þǣm mǣstum ġesǣlþum and on þǣre mǣstan weorþunge.

NOTES

23 g. **ġehierde** 'heard' preterite of *ġehīeran* 6. **ġesāwon** 'saw' preterite plural of *ġesēon.*

24 g. **grētte** 'greeted' preterite of *grētan.*

25 g. **ġeseah** preterite singular of *ġesēon* 23. **sēo undǣd** 'evil deed, crime', literally 'un-deed'; *sēo dǣd* 17. **feorran** 'from afar'.

26 g. **canst þū** 'knowest thou' from *cann.* **þisne** 62. **se cræft** 'art, trade, occupation'. **ġesihst** 'seest' from *ġesēon.*

27 g. **ealneweġ** 'always', literally 'all the way'; *se weġ* 'road, way'. **ġearo** 'ready'. **wunodon** 'dwelt' preterite plural of *wunian.* **þǣr** 'there'. **lang** 'long'. **sēo tīd** 'time'.

28 g. **sēo heall** 'hall'. **iernþ** 'runs' from *iernan* 2; *iernþ ymb* 'revolves round'. **sēo eorþe** 'earth' 8.

30 g. **sęle** 'give!' from *sęllan.* **se hafoc** 'hawk'. **hwæt** 'what'. **sċeal** 'shall'. **þīn** 'thy'. **ġebrōþru** plural of *brōþor* 11. **þæt hors** 'horse'.

31 g. **se god** 'God'. **sealde** preterite of *sęllan.* **þæt leoht** 'light'.

32 g. **se slǣp** 'sleep'. **biþ** 'is'. **se dēaþ** 'death'. **ġelīcost** 'most like' from *ġelīc.* **andswarode** preterite of *andswarian* 'answer', from *sēo andswaru* 1. **þus** 'thus'. **ġelīcode** 'pleased' from *ġelīcian.* **sēo cwēn** 'the queen'. **sind** 'are'. **ġetrīewe** 'faithful' plural of *getrīewe.*

33 g. **eall** 'all'. **nytt** 'useful'. **on-bestæl** 'stole on, came upon'; *stelan* 'steal'. **ċearf** 'cut' from *ċeorfan*. **þæt hēafod** 'head', plural *hēafdu*. **of** 'off'. **se fisċere** 'fisherman'. **breġdaþ** 'pull, twist, weave' from *breġdan*. **þæt nętt** 'net'.

34 g. **se dæġ** 'day, life-time'. **ēode** 'went' preterite of *gān*. **sēo strǣt** 'paved (Roman) road, street'. **wacian** 'to watch'. **se þēof** 'thief'. **sæt** 'sat' from *sittan*. **se ealdormann** 'chief, duke, nobleman'. **cwæþ** 'spoke, said' from *cweþan*.

35 g. **se mangere** 'merchant'. **ā·stāg** 'ascended' from *ā·stīgan*. **se bēam** 'tree'. **hangiaþ** 'hang' from *hangian*. **se męre** 'lake'. **ūte** 'outside, out'. **sēo sǣ** 'sea'. **se bāt** 'boat' —*on ānum bāte* 'in a boat'; *ān* 'one' is also used as an indefinite article, which is, however, generally omitted.

37 g. **nān** 'no one, none' is also used as an adjective, as in *nān mann* 'no man'. **of·slōg** 'killed' from *of·slēan*. **þrītiġ** 'thirty'.

38 g. **se steorra** 'star'. **sēo hǣte** 'heat'.

39 g. **bętst** 'best' from *gōd*; compare *bętera* 'better'.

40 g. **mǣrost** 'most famous' from *mǣre*.

41 g. **ġemunde** 'remembered' from *ġeman*. **þæt word** 2. **þe** 'which'. **ǣr** 'formerly, before'. **spræc** 'spoke' from *sprecan*. **þæt yfel** 'evil'. **wēnan** 'to expect, hope'. **fæġnian** 'rejoice'. **se ġebēorsċipe** 'feast'; *se ġebēor* 'boon-companion', literally 'fellow beer-drinker', where the *ġe-* gives the sense of 'together', as in *ġefēra* 'companion', originally 'fellow-traveller' (*fēran* 'go, travel') and *ġebrōþru* 30; but in many words the *ġe-* has no meaning.

42 g. **þæt sweord** 3. **on·fōn** 'to receive'; *fōn* 91. **se męte** 'food'. **brūcan** 'enjoy'. **fiend** plural (18) of *se fēond* 9. **ehtan** 'to pursue, persecute'.

43 g. se friþ 'peace'. **bǣdon** 'prayed, asked' from *biddan*.

44 g. ġetiþode 'granted' from *ġetiþian*. **þancode** 'thanked' from *þancian*. **þæs** genitive of *þæt* 'that, it'.

46 g. se strand 'shore'.

48 g. se wita 'sage, councillor'.

49 g. se cræft 26. **þæt ċild** 11. **sēo cwēn** 32.

50 g. sum 'a certain, a, some', used also as a noun 'a certain one, some one'.

51 g. se middanġeard 6. **þæt mōd** 'courage'. **wunode** preterite of *wunian* 27. **ġedafenaþ** 'befits' from *ġedafenian*. **sīe** 'be, is' subjunctive. **cystiġ** 'liberal'. **dīeġle** 'secret, hidden'. **sēo stōw** 'place'. **sēo þearf** 'need'. **þrēo** 'three'. **þæt pund** 'pound'. **sēo butere** 'butter.' **swift** 'swift'. **se hund** 7. **nīwe** 'new.' **cūþ** 'known' adjective. **þæt ġemōt** 'meeting'—*ealra witena* (48) *ġemōt* 'parliament'.

52 g. sprec imperative of *sprecan* 41. **milde** 'mild, gentle, kind'. **se munuc** 'monk'. **gāþ** 'go' from *gān* 34. **ǣlċ** 'each'. **se nīþ** 'enmity, violence'.

57 g. þæt mæġen 'strength'. **hēold** 'held' from *healdan*. **fīftiġ** 'fifty'. **se winter** 'winter', in reckoning 'year'. **se cęmpa** 5.

58 g. se lārēow 9. **wille, willaþ** 'will' from *willan*. **þæt** 'that' conjunction. **dō** 'do' from *dōn*. **lǣre** 'teach' from *lǣran*.

59 g. wæs 'was'. **Dęne** only in plural 'Danes'; the names of nations are used also for the country itself, so that *on Dęnum* 'in or among the Danes' means also 'in Denmark'. **hāten** 'named, called' from *hātan*. **āsċode** 'asked' from *āsċian*. **be** 34 is used also in the sense of 'about, concerning'.

60 g. āgen 'own'.

62 g. hwanon 'whence'. **cōmon** 'came' from *cuman*. **hider** 'hither'. **þæt land** 'land, country, land as opposed to water'. **swīþe** 'severely, excessively, very'. **brād** 'broad'. **sēo niht** 'night'. **þæt þing** 'thing, affair'.

63 g. **dyde** 'did' from *dōn* 58. **hū** 'how'. **mæġ** 'can'. **bēon** 'to be'. **ġesǣliġ** 'happy'. **ġesǣlþa** feminine plural 'happiness, prosperity'. **þurh·wunian** 'to continue, remain'; *þurh* 'through', *wunian* 27. **mōt** 'may'.

64 g. **hwider** 'whither'; compare *hider* 62. **wilt** 'wilt' from *willan* 58.

65 g. **cōmon** 62. **sċēawian** 'look at, reconnoitre'. **fæġer** 'beautiful'. **on** 'on' is here used as an adverb; compare *on bestæl* 33. **lōcian** 'look'.

66 g. **rīdan** 'ride'.

88 g. **healdan** 'hold, possess 57, preserve, guard'. **ælmihtiġ** 'almighty'.

89 g. **nū** 'now'. **fūs** 'hastening, ready to start'. **se eard** 'native country'. **sēċan** 'seek 83, visit'.

90 g. **hwæt** 'what' 30, here 'who'. **mihton** preterite (84) of *mæġ* 63. **ā·þęnċan** 'think out, devise'; compare *þęnċan* 83. **wiþ·standan** 'withstand, resist'.

91 g. **bæd** preterite of *biddan, hē bitt* (70), *hē bæd, hīe bǣdon* (43), *ġebeden.* **se fultum** 'help'. **belīfan,** *belāf, belifon* 'remain'. **bæftan** 'behind.' **ūþe** preterite (84) of *ann* 'grant'. **mōste** preterite (84) of *mōt* 63. **inn** adverb 'in'. **þæt pleoh** 'danger'. **man** indefinite pronoun 'one'; formed from *se mann.* **se hwæl** 'whale'. **fōn,** *fēhþ, fēng, ġefangen* 'seize, catch, take'—*þæt man ġefō* 'to catch'. **swā** 'so 9, as'; **hwelċ** 'who, which'—*swā hwelċ swā* 'whoever'. **begā** imperative of *begān* 'practice'; *gān* 64.

92 g. **rīċsian** 'rule'; *þæt rīċe* 57. **swelċe** adverb 'as if'; *swelċ* 'such'. **næs nā** 'was not'.

93 g. **ġif** 'if'. **unforht** 'intrepid'; *forht* 'afraid, timid'. **swā . . swā** 'so . . as' 91. **self** 'self'. **neart** 'art not'.

95 g. neom 'am not'. **spēdiġ** 'rich'. **þæt wīn** 2. **bycgan** 'buy.' **dēoplicor** adverb, comparative of *dēoplīċe* 'deeply'; *dēop* 'deep'. **þonne** 'than'. **ā·beran** 'carry, support, endure'.

97 g. þæt ġielpword 'boastful word or speech, vaunt'; *þæt word* 41; 13 (gender). **þæt będd** 'bed'. **stīgan**, *stāg*, *stigon* 'ascend'; compare *ā·stīgąn* 35.

98 g. wundorliċ 'wonderful'. **þynċan** 'seem'. **nis** 'is not'. **nān-þing** neuter 'nothing'; *þæt þing* 62. **būtan** 'except, but'. **sēo sċeado** 'shadow, shade'.

106 g. ēow is here dative. **wīsian**, *wīsode* 'guide'; *sēo wīse* 'manner, way'. **sōna** 'immediately, quickly, soon', the last meaning being only occasional.

107 g. of·slēan 37; *slēan*, *slihþ*, *slōg*, *slæġen* 'strike, slaughter'.

108 g. se wyrhta 'worker, workman, artificer'; *wyrċan* 83. **ġesamnian**, *ġesamnode* 'collect, gather'. **sēo wund** 'wound'. **nǣfre** 'never'. **hǣlan** 'heal'. **se dęmm** 'injury'. **maniġ** 'many'. **fram** preposition with dative 'from, by'. **se sǣmann** 'sailor, pirate'.

110 g. feallan, *fielþ*, *fēoll*, *ġefeallen* 'fall'.

1. be 59 g. **þissum** 62 g. **se middanġeard** 51 g. **sēo sunne** 4 g. **gǣþ** 103 g. **betwēonan** 'between' preposition with dative. **se heofon** 'sky, Heaven' 8 g. **sēo eorþe** 28 g. **on dæġ** 15 g, 35 g 'by day, in the daytime'; *dæġ* here is not the accusative, but an old form of the dative. **bufan** 'above' preposition with dative. **on niht** 62 g. **under** 35 g. **ǣfre** 'always, ever'; compare *nǣfre* 109 g. **biþ** 102 g, 106 g. **iernan** 28 g, *arn*, *urnon* 'run, flow'. **ymb** prep. w. acc. 28 g. **and** 'and'. **ealswā**, in which the *eal-* is *eall* 33 g used as an adverb, and **swā-swā** have the same meaning as the simple *swā* 91 g, so that *ealswā* . . *swā-swā* is equivalent to *swā* . . *swā* 93 g. **leohte** adverb 'brightly' from *leoht* 'bright'; compare *þæt leoht* 31 g. **sċīnan,** *sċān, sċinon* 'shine': **dēþ** 103 g. **ūrum** 60 g. **hēafdum** 33 g.

2. sēo healf 'side, quarter, direction'. **þe** is not only a relative pronoun 63 g, but also a relative adverb with a variety of meanings, here 'where, in which'. **þǣr** 27 g refers back to *on þā healfe.* **ne** 109 g.

3. hātan, *hǣtt, hēt, hāten* 59 g 'call, name, command, bid, ask'. **ān** 2 g. **fram** 108 g. **se ūpgang** 'going up, rising'. **oþ** 'until, up to' preposition with accusative. **se ǣfen** 'evening'. **oþ-þæt** conjunction 'until', literally 'until that (that)'. **eft** adverb 'again, (come) back, afterwards'. **becuman** 67 g—*eft becuman* 'return'; 97 g (mood). **þǣr** 'to the place where'. **ǣr** 41 g. **ūp** 'upwards, up'. **stāg** 97 g. **þæt fæc** 'space of time, period'. **sind** 102 g. **tęllan,** *tęlþ, tealde* 'count, consider (to be so and so)'. **fēower** 'four'. **twentiġ** 'twenty'. **sēo tīd** 'time, hour' 27 g, 57 g (case).

4. swīþe 62 g. **miċel** 51 g. **brād** 62 g. **þæs-þe** 'according as, as' is made up of *þæs* 59 g and the adverb *þe* 2. **bēċ** 18 g. **sęcgan,** *sęġþ, sæġde,* imperative *sęġe* 'say' 71 g, 83 g, 100 g. **se ymbhwyrft** 'circuit'; *ymb* 1, *hweorfan* 10. **ac** 'but'. **þynċan,** *þuhte* 98 g, 84 g. **lȳtel** 2 g, 50 g (ending). **for·þǣmþe** or **for·þǣm** 'because', literally 'for that (that)'; *for* 34 g, *þǣm* 59 g, *þe* 2. **feorr** adverb 'far'; compare *feorran* 25 g. **sēo ġesihþ** 'power of sight, what is seen'; compare *hē ġesihþ* 'sees'.

5. mōna, steorra 38 g. **on·fōþ** 42 g; **fōn** 91 g. **þæt leoht** 31 g.

6. sęttan 82 g 'set, appoint'. **mannum** 33 g (case). **tō** 34 g 'to', here 'for'. **sēo ręst** 'rest, bed'. **þēah-þe** 98 g.

þynċe 98 g (mood). **þæt mancynn** 'mankind'; *se mann, þæt cynn* 'species, race, lineage'.

7. **dæġhwǣmlīċe** 'daily' adverb; *se dæġ, hwǣm* 61 g (compare *ġehwā* 'each'), *-līċe* (compare *dēoplīċe* 95 g). **weaxan,** *wiext, wēox, ġeweaxen* 'grow, increase, wax'. **wanian,** *wanode* 79 g 'decrease, wane'. **simle** 'continually, always'. **węndan,** *węnt, węnde* 70 g 'turn (transitive and intransitive), go'. **se hrycg** 'back'.

8. **þæt ġēar** 'year'. **twelf** 'twelve'. **se mōnaþ** 'month'. **twā** 56 g. **fīftiġ** 57 g. **sēo wuce** 'week'. **siextiġ** 'sixty'; *siex* 'six'. **daga,** the noun is usually repeated in this way after the smaller number. **tō·ēacan** preposition with dative 'besides'; *tō* and *se ēaca* 'increase'—*þǣr-tōēacan* 'in addition to that'. **tīda** nominative.

9. **se reġn** 'rain'. **cuman** 64 g, *cymþ* 73 g, *cōm, cumen.* **of** preposition with dative 'from, of': also adverb 'off' 33 g. **sēo lyft** 'air'. **ā·tēon** = *tēon, tīehþ, tēah, tugon, ġetogen* 'pull, draw'. **se wǣta** 'moisture'. **sē** 46 g. **gaderian,** *ge-* 41 g 'collect'. **se sċūr** 'shower'. **þonne . . þonne** 'when .. then'; demonstrative adverbs are used also relatively: *þā* 'then, when', *þǣr* 'there, where'. **māre** neuter (53 g) of *mara* 'bigger, greater, more' irregular comparative of *miċel.* **ā·beran** 95 g; *beran, bierþ, bær, bǣron, boren* 'carry, bring forth (child)'. **feallan** 110 g. **of dūne** 'down', literally 'from the hill (*sēo dūn*)'.

10. **se hagol** 'hail'. **se dropa** 'drop'. **frēosan,** *frēas, fruron, ġefroren* 'freeze'; compare *hrēosan* 75 g. **uppe** 'up'. **sōna** 106 g. **swā-swā** 1. **sum** 50 g. **se sċop** 'poet'. **ġieddian,** *ġieddode* 'compose or recite poetry'. **hwītost** superlative of *hwīt* 'white'. In reading these verses the words preceded by (·) must be uttered with extra stress. **þæt corn** 'grain, corn'. **hweorfan,** *hwierfþ, hwearf, hwurfon,*

ġehworfen 'turn, wander, proceed'; compare *ymbhwyrft* 4, and, for the inflections, *weorþan* 77 g. **hit** refers to *corn* understood. **wealcan,** *wēolc* 'roll, whirl'. **se wind** 'wind'. **wierþ** 77 g. **þæt wæter** 'water'. **siþþan** 'afterwards, then', also conjunction 'after, when'.

11. þe . . on 'in which'; *on* is here rather an adverbial prefix to the verb than a preposition. **libban,** *hē leofaþ, leofode* 'live'; compare *habban*, imperative *hafa* 104 g. **fēower** 3 g. **sēo ġesċeaft** 'created thing, element'. **nis** 109 g. **næbbe** = *ne hæbbe*, 95 g (mood). **mid** 34 g; prepositions sometimes follow the word they govern. **þæt fȳr** 'fire'.

12. þynne 'thin'. **ofer'gān** 'go over, pervade'. **ūp-stīgan** = *ūp-āstīgan* 3. **flēogan,** *flēag, flugon, ġeflogen* 'fly'. **se fugol** 'bird'. **se fisċ** 'fish'. **swimman,** *swamm, swummon* 'swim'. **mihte** subjunctive 93 g. **hira nān** 37 g. **nǣre** = *ne wǣre*, here 'if it were not for'. **þe** 63 g. **þæt wolcen** 'cloud'. **se stórm** 'storm'.

13. ā'styrian = *styrian, styrede* 'stir, disturb'. Observe the distinction between **is** and **biþ** 106 g.

14. se cræft 26 g. **hwelċ** 91 g. **canst** 84 g. **munuc** 52 g.

15. þās þīne ġefēran 'these ones (who are) thy companions'; *se ġefēra* 41 g. **se ierþling** 'agriculturist, farmer, ploughman'. **þæt sċēap** 'sheep'. **se hierde** 'herdsman, cowherd'. **þæt hrīþer** 'head of cattle'. **se hunta** 20 g. **se fisċere** 33 g. **se fuglere** 'fowler'; *se fugol* 12. **se ċiepemann** 'merchant'; *ċīepan* 'trade, buy, sell'. **se sċōh,** plural *sċōs* 47 g 'shoe'. **se wyrhta** 108 g. **se sealtere** 'salter, salt-maker'; *þæt sealt* 'salt'. **se bæcere** 'baker'.

16. seġst 4. **hū** 63 g. **begǣst** 91 g, 103 g. **lā** 'oh!', **lēof** 53 g—*lā lēof* or simply *lēof* '(dear) sir!'. **þearle** 'severely, very'. **swincan,** *swanc, swuncon* 'labour, suffer hardship'.

ǣlċe dæġe 52 g. **sċeal** 30 g, *þū sċealt, wē sċulon, hē sċolde* 'have to, ought to, shall'. **þæt dæġred** 'dawn'. **ūt** 'out'. **þonne** 'then' 9. **se oxa** 'ox'. **felda** dative of *se feld* 'field'. **drīfan**, *drāf, drifon* 'drive'. **sēo sulh** 7 g, plural *sylh* 18 g; nouns that form their nominative plural by vowel-change have the same form for the dative singular; so also *on þǣre byriġ* 'in the city'. **ġeocian**, *ġeocode* 'yoke'; *þæt ġeoc* 'yoke'. **nis nān** 109 g. **winter** 57 g. **stearc** 'severe'. **dearr**, *þū dearst, wē durron, dorste*, subj. pres. *dyrre* 'dare', 95 g (mood). **se hām** 'home'; **æt** preposition with dative 'at'—in *æt hām, hām* is an old dative 1. **lūtian**, *lūtode* 'skulk, hide'; *lūtan, lēat* 'bow, bend' intrans. **se hlāford** 7 g. **se ęġe** 'fear'. **ac** 4. **þæt sċear** 'ploughshare'. **se culter** 'coulter'. **fæstnian**, *fæstnode* 'fasten, confirm'; *fæst* 'firm'. **full** 'full'. **se æcer** '(ploughed) field, acre'. **ęrian**, *ęrede* 'plough'. **oþþe** 'or'. **māre** 9.

17. **ǣniġ** 'any'. **ġiese** 'yes'. **se cnapa** 5 g. **sēo gād** 'goad'. **þīen** *þīede* 'stab, pierce, drive'. **hās** 'hoarse'. **for** 34 g. **se ċiele** 'chill, cold'. **se hrēam** 'shouting'.

18. **dēst** 103 g. **ġiet** 'yet, still, in addition'. **tō dōnne** 65 g. **lēof** 16. **sēo binn** 'manger'. **þæt hīeġ** 'hay'. **ā-fyllan** 'fill'; *ġefyllan* 71 g 'fill, satisfy with food'. **wæterian**, *wæterode* 'water, make to drink'. **se steall** 'stall, stable'. **feormian**, *feormode* 'clean'.

19. **ēalā** 'ah!, oh'; *lā* 16. **þæt ġedeorf** 'labour, hardship'. **for-þǣm-þe** 4. **neom** 109 g. **frēo** 'free'.

20. **on ǣrnemerġen** 'early in the morning'; *ǣr* 41 g, *se morgen*, gen. *morgennes* 'morning'. **sēo lǣs**, plural *lǣswa* 'pasture'. **siþþan** 10. **standan**, *stęnt, stōd, gestanden* 'stand'. **se hund** 7 g. **þȳ-lǣs-þe** conjunction 'lest'; *lǣs* is the adverb of *lǣssa* 9 g. **se wulf** 'wolf'. **for-swelgan** 'devour'; *swelgan, swealg, swulgon, ġeswolgen* 'swallow'.

ǣfen 3. **lǣdan** 81 g. **on·ġēan** 'again, back'. **þæt loc** 'lock, bolt', plural *locu* 'sheepfold'. **meolcan,** *mealc* 'milk'. **tuwa** 'twice'. **macian,** *macode* 'make'. **sēo butere** 51 g. **se ċiese** 'cheese'. **ġetriewe** 32 g.

21. **on·ġeocian** 'unyoke'. **ealle niht** 27 g. **wacian,** *wacode* 'be awake, watch'. **for þēofum** 34 g. **þæs on morgenne** 'next morning'. **betǣċan** 'entrust, commit'; *tǣċan* 'show' 82 g. **eft** 3. **wel** 'well'. **ġefylde** 18.

22. **of** 9. **ǣniġ** 17. **þing** 98 g.

25. **hwæs** 61 g. **cyning** 15 g.

26. **breġdan** 33 g, *bræġd, brugdon, ġebrogden.* **nętt** 33 g. **ā·sęttan** = *sęttan* 82 g. **ġehæp** 'suitable'. **stōw** 51 g. **tyhtan** 'incite'. **hund** 20. **þæt wildēor** 'wild beast'. **ehtan** 42 g, preterite *ehte,* 91 g (mood). **oþ-þæt** 3. **on unġearwe** 'unawares'; *ġearo,* plur. *ġearwe* 27 g. **becuman** 3. **þus** 32 g. **læċċan,** *læhte* 'seize, take'. **þonne . . þonne** 9. **tō** is here adverb—'I come up'. **ofslēan** 107 g.

27. **būtan** preposition with dative 'without'; also adverb, conjunction 'except 6, unless'. **huntian,** *huntode* 'hunt'.

28. **fōn** 91 g. **swift** 51 g.

29. **swiþost** 'chiefly' adverb, superl. of *swiþe* 4. **se heorot** 'deer, stag'. **se rā** 'roebuck'. **se bār** 'wild boar'. **hwīlum** 'sometimes'—dat. plur. of *sēo hwīl* 'while, period of time'; compare *styċċemǣlum* 5 g. **se hara** 'hare'.

30. **tō·dæġ** 'to-day'; compare *on dæġ* 1. **se huntoþ** 'act of hunting, what is taken in hunting, game'. **nese** 'no'. **for·þǣm** 4. **se sunnan-dæġ** 'Sunday'; *sunnan* gen. of *sēo sunne.* **ac** 16. **ġiestrandæġ** 'yesterday'.

31. **twēġen** 56 g.

32. **ofstician,** *-ode* 'stab to death'; compare *ofslēan* 26.

33. **ġedyrstiġ** 'daring'; *dearr* 16. **bedrīfan** = *drīfan* 16.

fæstlīċe 'firmly'; *fæst* 16. **on·ġēan** 'against, to meet', also 'again' 20. **fǣrlīċe** 'suddenly'. **þæt spere** 'spear'.

34. þā 'then', also 'when' rel. 9. **forhtmōd** 'timid'; *forht* 93 g, *þæt mōd* 'mood, heart, mind, disposition, character, courage 51 g'. **missenliċ** 'various'. **wunian** 79 g. **se wudu** 'forest', nom. plur. and dat. sing. *wuda*; compare *se sunu, þā suna* 19 g.

35. ymb 1 'around, concerning, with regard to'. **huntoþ** 30. **sęllan,** *sęlþ, sealde,* imper. *sęle!* 83 g, 100 g. **swā hwæt swā** 'whatever'; *swā hwelċ swā* 91 g.

36. sċrȳdan 'clothe'; *þæt sċrūd* 'dress'. **fēdan,** *hē fētt, fēdde* 70 g. **hwīlum** 29. **þæt hors** 30 g. **oþþe** 16. **se bēag** 'ring, torque'; *būgan, bēag, bugon, ġebogen* 'bend, bow'. **þȳ** instrumental of *se*, as adverb 'the'; so also *hwȳ* 'why' is the instrumental of *hwā, hwæt.* **ġeornor** adverb, comparative of *ġeorne* 'eagerly, zealously' (*ġeorn* 'eager, willing').

38. beġietan, *beġiett, beġeat, beġēaton, beġieten* 'acquire, get'. **of** 9. **se bīleofa** 'sustenance'; *libban, leofode* 11. **þæt sċrūd** 36. **þæt feoh** 47 g.

39. se bāt 35 g. **rōwan,** *rēow* 'row'. **ūt** 16. **sēo ēa** 46 g. **weorpan,** *wearp, wurpon, ġeworpen* 'throw'. **se angel** 'hook'. **þæt ǣs** 'carrion, bait'. **sēo spyrte** 'basket'. **hæftan** 'seize, take'. **niman,** *nam, nāmon, ġenumen* 'take'.

40. ġif 93 g. **unclǣne** 'impure'; *clǣne* 'clean, pure'. **se męte** 42 g.—*mē tō męte* 6.

41. hwǣr 'where'. **ċiepan,** *ċiepte* 15. **ċeaster** 17 g.

42. bycgan 95 g, *byġþ, bohte* 83 g. **ċeasterware** 'citizens'; compare *Dęne* 59 g. **hira** 37 g. **fela** 29. **sęllan** 60.

43. se ǣl 'eel'. **se hacod** 'pike'. **sēo sċēote** 'trout'; *sċēotan, sċiett, sċēat, sċuton, sċoten* 'shoot, dart' trans. and intr. **ōþer** 'other'. **ēam** 46 g. **swimman** 12.

44. for·hwȳ 'for what, why'; *hwȳ* 36. **fisċian,** *fisċode* 'fish'. **sǣ** 46 g. **dō** 103 g. **seldon** 'seldom.' **mē** 33 g. **þæt rēwett** 'rowing'; *rōwan.*

45. **se hæring** 'herring'. **se leax** 'salmon'. **se styria** 'sturgeon'. **sēo lopestre** 'lobster'. **se crabba** 'crab'. **ōþerra** 43; *fela* always governs the genitive.

46. **wilt** 105 g. **hwæl** 91 g. **niċ** 'not I' is an emphatic 'no'.

47. **for·hwȳ** 44. **þæt pleoh** 91 g. **lǣsse** 9 g, 53 g. **þonne** 95 g. **se hwælhuntoþ** 30. **faran,** *færþ, fōr, ġefaren* 'go, travel'.

48. **lēofre** 53 g. **ofslēan** 26. **nealles þæt ān . . ac** 'not only . . but'; *nealles* 'not at all, not', *ealles* 'entirely' (gen. of *eall*); observe that *ān* keeps its strong form after the definite article to distinguish it from the weak *āna* 'alone, only'. **self** 93 g. **ēac swelċe** 'also'; *ēac* 'also'; *swelċe* 92 g has here its other meaning 'like' (compare our *likewise* = 'also'). **se slęge** 'stroke'; *slēan* 107 g. **besęnċan**=*sęnċan, sęnċte* 'sink' trans.; *sincan, sanc* 'sink' intrans. **oþþe** 36.

49. **þēah** 'yet, however', also 'though, although' 98 g. **sēo frēċennes** 'danger'; *frēċne* 'dangerous'. **æt·berstan** 'escape'; *berstan, bierst, bærst, burston* 'burst'. **se sċeatt** 'money, profit'. **þanon** 'thence'; compare *hwanon* 62 g. **beġietan** 38. **þæt sōþ** 8 g 'truth'; *sōþ* 'true'. **þæt mōd** 34. **sēo slǣwþ** 'sloth'; *slǣw* 'sluggish.'

50. **beswīcan,** *beswāc, beswicon, beswicen* 'deceive, get the better of'. **se fugol** 12. **maniġfeald** 'manifold, various'. **sēo wīse** 106 g. **þæt grīn** 'snare'. **sēo træppe** 'trap'. **se līm** 'paste, mortar, birdlime'. **sēo wistlung** 'whistling'; *wistlian* 'whistle.' **se·hafoc** 30 g.

51. **ġiese** 17.

52. **tęmian,** *tęmede* 'tame'; *tam* 'tame.' **nytt** 33 g. **būtan** 27. **cūþe** subjunct. 93 g.

53. lustlīċe 'willingly'; *se lust* 'pleasure, desire'. **māra** 9. **hwæþer** 'whether'—*hwæþer-þe* 'or'.

54. ā·fēdan = *fēdan* 36. **wintra** dative of *se winter* 16. **ġe** 'and'. **ēac swelċe** 48. **se lęnċten** 'spring, Lent'. **lǣtan**, *lǣtt, lēt, lǣten* 'let'. **wuda** 34. **æt·flēogan** 'fly away'; compare *æt·berstan* 49. **mē** 33 g. **niman** 39. **se bridd** 'young bird'. **se hærfest** 'autumn'.

55. nyle = *ne wile*. **se sumor** 'summer', dat. *sumera*; compare *wintra* 54, *wuda* 34, *suna*. **þearle** 16. **etan** 73 g, *itt, ǣt, ǣton*.

56. ġearo 27 g. **swelċ** 92 g. **þæt ġeswinc** 'labour, trouble, hardship'; *swincan* 16. **nealles** 48.

57. se mangere 'merchant' = *ċiepemann* 15. **nytt** 52. **se ealdormann** 34 g. **weliġ** 'rich'; *se wela* 'wealth'. **þæt folc** 16 g.

58. ā·stīgan 35 g, 97 g. **se hlæst** 'load, freight'. **faran** 47. **ofer sǣ** 35 g, *sǣ* accusative. **bycgan** 42. **dēorwierþe** 'precious'; *wierþe* 'worth, worthy, honoured'. **þæt land** 62 g. **ā·cęnnan** 'bring forth, produce'. **lǣdan** 81 g. **hider** 62 g. **plēo** 47, 47 g. **þolian**, *þolode* 'suffer, endure'. **sēo for·lidennes** 'shipwreck'; *līþan, lāþ, lidon, ġeliden* 'travel by water, sail'; compare *for·lēosan, -lēas, -luron, -loren* 'lose'. **losian**, *losode* 'be lost, perish, escape'; compare *for·lēosan*. **unēaþe** 'with difficulty, scarcely'; *ēaþe* 'easily'. **cucu** 'alive'. **æt·berstan** 49.

59. lǣtst 70 g. **se pæll** 'purple'. **se seoloc** 'silk'. **seld-cūþ** 'rare'; *seldon* 44, *cūþ* 51 g. **þæt rēaf** 'robe'. **þæt wyrt-ġemang** 'spice'; *sēo wyrt* 'plant, vegetable, herb'; *þæt ġemang* 'mixture' (compare *męnġan* 6 g). **þæt wīn** 2 g. **se ele** 'oil'. **þæt elpendbān** 'elephants' bone, ivory'. **se ġimm** 'gem'. **þæt gold** 13 g. **þæt tin** 'tin'. **se mæstling** 'brass'. **þæt ār** 'bronze'. **þæt seolfor** 'silver'. **þæt glæs** 'glass.'

60. wiþ prep. with acc. 'against, towards, to', with dat. 'in exchange for'. **sęllan wiþ weorþe** 'give for a price, sell'; hence *sęllan* by itself comes to mean 'sell'. **se ilca** 'the same.' **þe . . mid** 'with which'. **ūte** 'outside, out 35 g, abroad'. **nię** 46. **fręmman,** *fręmeþ, fręmede* 'perform, help, benefit, promote'. **þæt ġedeorf** 19. **þæt ġestrēon** 'gain, wealth'. **þæt wīf** 'woman 16 g, wife'. **þæt bearn** 'child'.

61. wyrċan 83 g 'work, make, do'. **sēo nytt** 'utility'. **niedbehēfe** 'necessary'; *sēo nīed* 'need'. **sēo hȳd** 'hide'. **þæt fell** 'skin'. **ġearcian,** *ġearcode* 'prepare'; *ġearo* 56. **missenliċ** 34. **þæt cynn** 6. **þæt ġesċȳ** 'boots and shoes'; *sċōh* 15. **sēo leþerhose** 'leather gaiter'. **se þwang** 'thong'. **þā ġerǣdu** neut. plur. 'harness'. **sēo flasċe** 'leather bottle'. **se fǣtels** 'pouch, bag'. **wunian,** *wunode* 34 'dwell, continue'. **būtan** 27.

62. ēalā 19. **fręmeþ** 60. **þæt flǣsċ** 'flesh'; **męttas** plur. of *se męte* 40. **brūcan** 42 g, *brēac, brucon.* **swētmęttas** 'dainties'; *swēte* 'sweet.' **þæt sealt** 15. **se swæcc** 'taste, flavour'. **ġefylþ** 21. **se cleofa** 'chamber, pantry'. **þæt hēdærn** 'storeroom'; *hēdan* 'heed, take care of', *þæt ærn* 'house'. **losaþ** 58. **būtan** 'unless'. **healdan,** *hiell, hēold, ġehealden* 'hold, preserve, protect' 88 g. **ne** 'not, nor'— *ne . . ne* 'neither . . nor'. **furþum** 'even'. **sēo wyrt** 59.

63. hwæþer (53) is sometimes used in direct questions, taking the subj. when the question is to be answered in the negative. **þæt līf** 'life'. **ā·drēogan** 'endure, pass (life), perform'; *drēogan, drīehþ, drēag, drugon,* 'endure'. **tō hwīle** 'for a time' 29. **nā** 92 g. **lange** adverb 'long', *lang* adject.; compare *leohte* 1, *swīþe* 4, *þearle* 16. **tō** 'too, very'. **wel** 21. **ǣlċ** 16. **se bēod** 'table'. **ǣmettiġ** 'empty'. **ġeþuht** 4—*biþ ġeþuht* 'seems'. **se hlāf** 9 g. **se wlǣtta**

'nausea'. **hwierfan** 'turn' trans.; *hweorfan* 10. **strangian,** *strangode* 'strengthen'; *strang* 'strong'. **sēo heorte** 'heart'. **se wer** 'man (as opposed to woman)'. **þæt mæġen** 57 g. **ġe** 54. **furþum** 62. **se lȳtling** 'child'; *lȳtel.* **nyllaþ**=*ne willaþ.* **mē** dat. **for·þolian** 'dispense with'; *þolian, þolode* 58.

64. se cōc 'cook'. **sęcge wē**: when the pronoun immediately follows the verb, *-aþ* becomes *-e*; compare *wille ġit* 58 g. **hwæþer** 63, here with the indic. **tō āwihte** 'at all'; *āwiht* neut. 'anything'. **beþearf**=*þearf* 'need, require', *þū þearft, þurfon, þorfte*; *sēo þearf* 51 g. **se ġefērsċipe** 'community'; *se ġefēra.* **etaþ** 55. **grēne** 6 g. **hrēaw** 'raw'. **fætt** 'fat'. **þæt broþ** 'broth'.

65. rēċċan, *rēċþ, rohte* 'care for, heed'. **sēoþan,** *sēaþ, ġesoden* 'boil'. **brǣdan** 'roast'. **se þēow** 'slave, servant'. **þēah·hwæþre** 'nevertheless'.

66. þā ōþre: *ōþer* always strong. **wyrhta** 108 g. **munuc** 14. **ġesēon,** *-sihþ, -seah* (25 g), *-sāwon, -sewen.* **ēac** (48); w. dat. 'besides'. **þæt īsen** 'iron', also adjective. **smiþ** 13 g. **se trēowwyrhta** 'carpenter'; *trēow* 10 g.

67. wīs 9 g. **se ġeþeahtere** 'councillor, adviser, manager'. **ġewisslīċe** 'certainly'; *ġewiss* 'certain'; compare *fæstlīċe, fǣrlīċe* 33, *lustlīċe* 53. **wīssian,** *wissode* 'guide, manage'.

68. wīsa: the weak form is used to show the vocative relation. **fyrmest** 'first', adverb 'in the first place'. **ġeþuht** 63. **god** 31 g. **se þēowdōm** 'service', 65. **betweox** prep. with dat. 'between, among'. **Crist** 'Christ'. **þæt godspell** 'gospel'; *þæt spell* 'narrative, story'. **cweþan,** *cwæþ, cwǣdon, ġecweden* 'speak, say'. **sēċan** 83 g. **þæt rīċe** 16 g. **īeċan,** *īehte* 'increase'; *ēac.*

69. sēo woruld 'world'. **sēo eorþtilþ** 'agriculture'.

70. hwanon 62 g. **se āwel** 'awl'. **se sēamere** 'tailor';

se sēam 'seam'. **sēo nǣdl** 'needle'. **þæt ġeweorc** 'act of working, what is made or done'.

71. andswarian, *-ode* 58 g. **sōþ** 49. **wīcian,** *wīcode* 'lodge, dwell, encamp, anchor'. **se drynċe** 'drink'. **sēo smiþþe** 'smithy'. **īsen** 66. **se spearca** 'spark'. **bēatan,** *bēot* 'beat'. **se slęcg** 'sledge-hammer'; *slēan.* **se swēġ** 'sound'. **blāwan,** *blēow* 'blow'. **se byliġ** 'leather bag', plur. 'bellows'.

72. notian, *notode* 'enjoy, make use of'. **þæt fæt,** plur. *fatu* (compare *dagas*) 'vessel, dish'.

73. þæt þȳrel 'hole'; *þurh* prep. with acc. 'through'.

74. hrædlīċe 7 g. **ġesēman** 'reconcile, settle (dispute)'. **þæt ġeflit** 'dispute, rivalry, emulation'. **sīe** 102 g, 88 g (mood). **sēo sibb** 'peace, relationship'. **sēo ġeþwǣrnes** 'concord, tranquillity'; *ġeþwǣre* 'not at variance'. **betweox** 68. **fręmman** 60. **uton** 'let us!' **weorþian,** *weorþode* 'honour, respect'; *wierþe* 58. **se bīleofa** 38. **þæt fōdor** 'food, fodder'. **lǣran** 'teach' 58 g, 'advise' with dat. or acc. of the person. **se rǣd** 'advice, deliberation, resolution, policy, what is desirable, help'. **ānra-ġehwelċ** 'each'; *ġehwelċ* 'each'. **ġeornlīċe**=*ġeorne* 36. **sē-þe** 63 g. **for'lǣtan** 'leave, abandon'; *lǣtan* 54. **fram** 108 g. **swā hwelċ swā** 91 g. **sīe** 91 g (mood). **swā . . swā** 'whether . . or'. **se mæsse-prēost** 'mass-priest'; *sēo mæsse* 'mass,' *se prēost* 'priest'. **se ċeorl** 'free man of the lowest rank, plebeian'. **se cęmpa** 5 g. **þæt þæt** 'that which'. **se dęmm** 108 g. **sēo sċand** 'disgrace'. **nyle** 55. **sċeal** 16.

75. þæt ċild 11 g. **līcian,** *līcode* 32 g. **sēo sprǣc** 'talk, speech'; *sprecan* 76 g, *spricþ, spræc, sprǣcon.* **dēoplīċe** 95 g. **ofer** 'over' 35 g, 'beyond'. **sēo mǣþ** 'capacity'. **wiþ** 60. **æfter** 'after 34 g, according to'. **þæt andġiet** 'understanding, intellect'. **under'standan** 'understand'; *standan* 20.

76. āscian, *āscode* 90 g. **leornian,** *leornode* 'learn'. **nyllaþ** = *ne willaþ*; *nyle* 55. **stunt** 'stupid'. **þæt nīeten** 'animal'. **nyton** = *ne witon*. **þæt gærs** 6 g.

78. se wīsdōm 'wisdom'; compare *se þēowdōm* 68. **lytiġ** 'cunning'. **fācenfull** 'treacherous'; *þæt fācen* 'treachery'. **þæt yfel** 41 g. **þenċan** 83 g. **se byrġels** 'tomb'. **wiþ·ūtan** 'outside'. **fæger** 65 g. **wiþ·innan** 'inside'. **fūl** 'foul'. **sēo licettung** 'hypocrisy'. **beswīcan** 50.

79. bilewit 'innocent, simple'. **for·būgan** 'avoid'; *būgan* 36. **þæt gōd** 'goodness, good thing'. **þēah·hwæþre** 65. **giet** 18. **dēoplicor** 95 g; compare *ġeornor* 36. **sēo ieldo** 95 g. **ā·beran** 95 g, 9. **mæġe** 95 g (mood). **se ġewuna** 'habit'. **næs** 'not'.

80. ealswā 1. **biddan** 91 g. **se cnapa** 17. **tō·dæġ** 30. **niht** dat. 62 g—*on þisse niht* 'last night'. **þā-þā** 'when'= *þā* 34. **se cnyll** 'sound of bell'. **ā·rīsan,** *ā·rīst, ā·rās, ā·rison* 75 g. **þæt bedd** 97 g. **sēo ċiriċe** 5 g. **ēode** 103 g. **singan,** *sang, sungon, ġesungen* 'sing'. **se uhtsang** 'matins'; *se uht* 'time just before dawn', *se sang* 'song'. **ġebrōþru** 'brothers 30 g, monks'. **se hālga** 6 g; *hāliġ* 6 g. **se lofsang** 'hymn'; *þæt lof* 'praise'. **þæt prīm** 'prime'. **seofon** 'seven'. **se sealm** 'psalm'. **sēo letānie** 'litany'. **sēo capitolmæsse** 'first mass'. **sēo underntīd** 'tierce'; *se undern* 'nine in the morning', *tīd* 8. **se middæġ** 'midday'. **drincan,** *dranc, druncon, druncen* 'drink'. **slǣpan,** *slēp* 'sleep'. **þæt nōn** 'noon'. **nū** 89 g. **beforan** prep. with dat. 'before'.

81. hwonne 'when'. **se ǣfensang** 20. **se nihtsang** 'compline'. **se tīma** 'time'.

82. beswingan=*swingan, swang, swungon, ġeswungen* 'beat'. **nese** 30. **wærliċe** 'cautiously'; *wær* 'wary'. **iċ mē hēold** 'I behaved', 62.

83. hwæt 'what, why'. **sēo dīeġelnes** 'secret'; *dīeġle* 51 g. **yppan** 'reveal'; *uppe* 10. **ġehwelċ** 74.

84. þæt ǣġ 'egg', plural *ǣġru*. **sēo bēan** 'bean'. **sēo þancung** 'thanking, thankfulness'; *þancian, þancode* 'thank'. **sēo ġierd** 'rod'. **drohtian,** *drohtode* 'pass (life), remain, be'; *drēogan* 63.

85. ġīfre 'greedy'. **þonne** 'when 81, since (causal).' **beforan** 80, 11. **se swelgere** 'glutton'; *swelgan* 20. **þæt cynn** 61. **mettas** 62. **þæt mǣl** 'time, proper time, food-time, meal'.

86. þæt ealo 'ale'.

87. þæt wīn 95 g. **spēdiġ** 95 g. **se drynċe** 71. **dysiġ** 'foolish'.

88. slǣpan 80. **þæt slǣpærn** 'dormitory'; compare *þæt hēdærn* 62.

89. ā·weċċan=*weċċan, weċþ, weahte* 'wake'. **se lārēow** 58 g. **stīþliċe** 'severely'; *stīþ* 'stiff, severe'. **sēo ġierd** 84.

90. manian, *manode* 'exhort'. **godcund** 'divine'. **sēo lār** 'what is taught, doctrine, advice'; *lǣran* 74. **ġehīersumian,** *-ode* 'be obedient to'; *ġehīersum* 'obedient', from *ġehīeran*. **ġerisenliċe** 'suitably, decorously'. **ġebǣran** 'bear oneself, behave'; *beran*. **sēo stōw** 26. **sēo belle** 'bell'. **þēawliċe** 'properly'; *se þēaw* 'custom, habit', *þēawas* 'conduct, virtue'. **þæt ġebed** 'prayer'; *ġebiddan* 'pray', *biddan* 80. **būgan** 36. **ēaþmōdliċe** 'humbly'; *ēaþmōd* 'humble'. **þæt wēofod** 'altar'. **ānmōdliċe** 'unanimously'; *ānmōd* 'of one (*ān*) mind (*mōd*)'. **sēo synn** 'sin'. **sēo hyġelīest** 'levity'; *hyġelēas* 'thoughtless'. **þæt clauster** 'cloister'. **sēo leornung** 'learning, study', 76.

91. se sīþ 'expedition'. **Dene** 59 g. **ġelimpan,** *ġelamp* 'happen'. **ġēo** 'formerly'. **hāten** 3. **se Hrōþgār** 'the (above-mentioned) Hroþgar'. **māre** 40 g. **se heretoga**

'general'; *se hęre* 'army', *-toga* from *tēon* 9. **se mǣg,** plural *māgas* 'kinsman'. **ġeorne** 36. **ġehīeran** 'hear, obey'. **oþ-þæt** 26. **se folgoþ** 'body of followers'; *folgian, folgode* 'follow'. **weaxan** 7. **se siġe** 'victory'. **hwider** 64g, 91g. **ǣġþer** 'each (of two)'—*ǣġþer ġe . . ġe* 'both . . and'.

92. sōna 10; *sōna swā* 'as soon as'. **fōn** (28) **tō rīċe** (68) 'succeed to the throne'. **samnian** 108g. **sēo fierd** 'army'; *faran* 47. **fīend** 90g. **sēċan** 68 'seek, attack'. **āgen** 60g. **swīþe** 62g. **for·slēan** 'slaughter'; *slēan* 107g. **for·dōn** 'destroy'. **oþ** (3) is here a conjunction 'until'. **unġemetliċ** 'excessive'; *þæt unġemet* 'excess', *þæt ġemet* 'measure, moderation, what is right'. **se ęġe** 16. **fram** 3.

93. þā 34. **sęndan,** *sęnt, sęnde* 81g 'send'. **se ǣrendraca** 'messenger, ambassador'; *þæt ǣrende* 'errand, message'. **friþes** 43g. **ġetīþian** 44g. **on þæt ġerād þæt** 'on condition of'. **þæt gafol** 'tribute'; *ġiefan*. **ġieldan,** *ġeald, guldon* 'pay'. **him tō hlāforde** 'to be their lord'. **ċēosan,** *ċēas, curon, ġecoren* 'choose'. **ġelǣstan** 'perform, carry out'. **se ġīsel** 'hostage'. **se āþ** 'oath'. **man** 91g. **se frēondsċipe** 'friendship'. **fæstnian** 16. **þæt wędd** 'pledge'. **ǣġþer** 91. **sēo healf** 2.

94. ā·swęrian=*swęrian, swōr, ġesworen* 'swear'. **węndan** 7. **on·ġēan** 20. **ġefēon,** *ġefeah, ġefǣgon, ġefæġen* 'rejoice'; *ġefæġen* has an active sense 'rejoicing'. **siþþan** 10. **sēo ġeþwǣrnes, sēo sibb** 74.

95. timbran, *timbrede* 'build'. **be·iernan**=*iernan* 1. **þæt mōd** 34—*bearn him on mōde* 'it occurred to him, he thought of'. **sēo heall** 39g. **þǣr·inne** 'in it', literally 'there inside'. **dǣlan** 'divide'; *se dǣl* 'part'. **sēo hęrehȳþ** 'booty'; *se hęre* 91. **ǣr ġefēngon** 'had taken'; *ǣr* (41g) often makes a preterite into a pluperfect.

96. hēt 3. **bętst** 39g. **se cynestōl** 'capital', literally 'royal seat'. **bannan**, *bēonn* 'proclaim, summon'. **sēo þēod** 'people'. **under·þiedan** 'subdue'; *þēod.* **þæt weorc** =*ġeweorc* 76. **on·ġinnan**, *-gann*, *-gunnon*, *-gunnen* 'begin'.

97. **se fierst** 'space of time'. **mǣst** superlative of *miċel.* **fæġer** 78. **lōcian** 65g, *lōcode* 'look'. **ā·sċieppan**=*sċieppan*, *sċōp*, *sċæpen* 'create, appoint'; compare *sēo ġesċeaft* 11. **se nama** 23g.

98. **ā·lēogan** 'fail in (promise)'; *lēogan*, *lēag*, *lugon*, *gelogen* 'tell lie'. **þæt bēot** 'vow, boast'. **se ġebēorsċipe** 41g. **āh**, *wē āgon*, *hē ahte* 'possess'. **se māþm** 'precious thing, treasure'.

99. The first **þǣr**='there', the second='where'. **man** 93. **ġesēon** 66. **sēo bliss** 'happiness, merriment'. **eft** 'afterwards'. **sēo iermþ** 'misery'; *earm* 'poor, wretched'. **sēo hearpe** 'harp'. **se swēġ** 71. **se sċop** 10. **sēo frumsċeaft** 'creation'; *se fruma* 'beginning'. **ælmihtiġ** 88g. **worhte** 61. **ūtan** 'outside'. **ymb·licgan** 'surround'; *licġan*, *līþ*, *læġ*, *lāgon*, *ġeleġen* 'lie'. **sęttan** 6. **þæt leoht** 5. **þæt trēow** 66. **frætwian**, *frætwode* 'adorn'. **þæt gærs** 76. **sēo wyrt** 62. **þæt līf** 63. **cucu** 58. **sēo wiht** 'creature, thing'; compare *āwiht* 64. **ġeond·hweorfan** 'traverse'; *hweorfan* 10.

100. **þurh·wunian** 63g. **onsǣġe** 'assailing'. **unfǣle** 'evil, uncanny'; *fǣle* 'faithful, gentle'. **hātte** passive of *hātan* 91 'is or was called'. **būn**, *būde* 'dwell'. **sēo mearc** 'border'; *þæt mearcland* 'border or waste land', **þæt fæsten**, gen. *fæstennes* 'fortress'; *fæst.* **þæt fęnn** 'fen'. **on·middan** prep. with dat. 'in the midst of'. **sweart** 'black'. **se mōr** 'moor'.

101. **wǣre** 89g (mood). **þæt cynn** 6. **gram** 'angry'. **se wræcsīþ** 'exile'; *sēo wracu* 'exile', *se sīþ* 91. **ā·sęndan** 81g. **hēt** 96. **þæt wēsten**, gen. *wēstennes*, 'desert'. **feorr** 4 adverb with dat. **þanon** 49. **on·wacan**, *-wōc* 'awake, originate'. **se dweorg** 'dwarf'. **se ælf**, plur. *ielfe* (compare *Dęne*) 'elf, sprite'. **se eoton** 'giant'. **wiþ** 60. **winnan,** *wann, wunnon* 'fight, war'.

102. **þolian** 58. **ælċe dæġe** 16. **sēo þīestro** 'darkness' 19 g.

103. **rēþe** 'fierce'. **on unġearwe** 26. **him on-bestæl** 33 g; *stelan, stæl, stǣlon, stolen* 'steal'. **yfel** 79. **wēnan** 41 g. **ġenam** 39. **fęrian** 79 g. **hām** 'home(wards)', acc. of *hām* 16. **fæġnian,** *fæġnode* 'rejoice'; *ġefēon* 94. **se þēaw** 90. **se līchama** 'body'; *þæt līc* 'body, corpse'. **þæt blōd** 'blood'.

104. **þæs on morgenne** 21. **sēo hęrġung** 'ravaging, warfare'; *hęrġian* 'ravage, make war', *se hęre.* **cūþ** 51 g. **se wōp** 'weeping'; *wēpan, wēop* 'weep'. **ā·hębban** = *hębban, hōf, hafen* 'lift, raise, exalt'. **sēo hēofung** 'lamentation'. **sittan,** *sitt, sæt, sǣton, ġeseten,* imper. *site* 100 g. **unblīþe** 'sad'; *blīþe* 'cheerful, happy, kind, well-disposed'. **him** (33 g) is here pleonastic. **wānian,** *wānode* 'lament, bewail'. **sēo heardsǣlþ** 'hardship, misfortune'; compare *ġesǣlþa* 63 g. **þæt folc** 57.

105. **þæt spor** 'track'; *ġespyrian* 'track, follow up'. **sweotole** adv., from *sweotol* 'clear, distinct'. **ġesīene** 'visible'; *ġesēon.* **næs þāra nān þe** . . 'there was none of those who' = 'there was no one'. **strang** 'strong, severe'.

106. **lǣtan** 54—*ne lēt hē nā langne fierst* (97) *þæt hē eft ne cōm* 'he did not let a long time elapse that he did not come again—without coming again'. **ymb here** 'after'. **se wælsliht** 'slaughter'; *slēan, hē slihþ.* **fręmman** 60. **murnan,** *mearn, murnon* 'feel remorse, care, mourn'. **sēo fǣhþ** 'feud'.

107. **nolde** 109 g. **lęnġ** adv., compar. of *lange* 63. **ęlles-hwǣr** 'elsewhere'. **sęo rępt** 6. **se būr** 'chamber, cottage'. **ǣmettiġ** 63. **unnytt** 'useless' 52. **on þǣm** 'in that (state)'. **twelf** 'twelve'. **winter** plur. of *se winter* 57 g.

108. **wēnan** 'expect' 103, 'think'. **ā·tęllan** 'enumerate, tell'; *tęllan* 3. **se dęmm** 74. **tō·ēacan** 8. **maniġfeald** 50. **þæt yfel** 103. **drēogan** 63. **þearf** 64. **of·slæġenra** 48 g (inflect.). **sēo bōt** 'mending, remedy, compensation'. **æt** prep. w. dat. 'at, from'. **ġeþingian**, *-ode* 'make terms, be reconciled'. **wiþ** 60. **for·ġieldan** 'atone, requite, pay'; *ġieldan* 93. **riht** 'right'; *þæt riht* 'what is right, duty'.

109. **þæt wundor** 'wonder, miracle'. **āna** 48. **winnan** 101. **þæt fæc** 3. **rīcsian** 'rule'; *þæt rīċe.* **þæt cynesetl** 'throne'; *þæt setl* 'seat'; compare *cynestol* 96. **grētan** 24 g 'greet, meddle with, touch'. **sōna þæs** 'as soon as'. **dagian** 'dawn'. **ġewītan**, *ġewāt*, *ġewiton*, *ġewiten* 'depart'. **wilde** 'wild'.

110. **ā·þęnċan** 90 g. **ā·cræftan** 'devise'; *se cræft.* **wiþ·standan** 90 g. **se eard** 89 g. **on·ġinnan** 96. **smēagan** 'consider'. **rǣdliċ** 'advisable'; *se rǣd* 74. **beorgan**, *bearg*, *burgon*, *ġeborgen* 'preserve, save'. **for·dōn** 92.

111. **nāhwæþer** 'neither' pronoun—*nāhwæþer ne . . ne* 'neither . . nor'; compare *hwæþer* 53. **dēah**, *dugon*, *dohte* 'avail, be worth something, be good'. **þæt wīg** 'war'. **ġerǣdan** 'resolve'. **blōtan**, *blēot* 'offer sacrifice'; *þæt ġeblōt* 'sacrificing'. **se hearg** 'temple'. **hǣþen** 'heathen'. **ġewuna** 79. **sēo help** 'help'. **nā þȳ lǣs for** 'none the less for, in spite of': compare 20. **fēran** 'go, travel, proceed, act'; *faran*, *ġefēra.* **earm** 99. **slēan** 107 g. **hīenan** 'humiliate, bully, illtreat'.

112. **þæt lēoþ** 'poem'. **þæt norþland** 'northern land'. **brocian** 'afflict'; *brecan* 'break'.

113. **sēo þēod** 96. **þæt Swēoland** 'Sweden'. **Ġēatas** 'Goths'. **se þeġn** 'thane, soldier, brave man'. **se nefa**

'nephew'; also 'grandson'. **ēne** 5 g. **strang** 105, compar. *strengra*, superl. *strengest*. **þæt mæġen** 63. **se gripe** 'grasp'.

114. **sēo undǣd** 25 g. **hraþe** = *hrædlīċe* 74 — *hraþe þæs þe* 'as soon as'. **ġierwan**, *ġierede* 'prepare, dress, arm'; *ġearo*. **þā** 'when', here 'since' (causal). **sēo þearf** 51 g. **ċēosan** 93. **fīftiene** 'fifteen'. **se cempa** 74. **findan**, *fint*, *funde* (weak!), *gefunden* 'find'.

115. **se strand** 46 g. **wiste** 'knew (to be there)'. **sċūfan**, *sċēaf*, *sċufon* 'push'—*ūt sċūfan* 'launch'. **hereġeatwa** fem. plur. 'equipment, armour'; *se here*. **se seġel** 'sail'. **ambyre** 'favourable (wind)'. **wīcian** 71. **siġlan** 'sail'. **furþor** 'further'. **þæt clif** 'cliff'. **hwit** 10. **se weall** 'wall'.

116. **tugon** 9. **þæt sand** 'sand'. **þancian**, *þancode* 44 g. **þæs þe** 'for that that, for' 44 g. **ġesund** 'safe and sound'. **þider** 'thither'. **bringan**, *brohte* 'bring' 83 g.

117. **se weard** '(coast)guard, sentinel'; *sēo weard* 'guarding, guard'. **se þeġn** 113. **ūp-gān** 'go up, land'. **mid wǣpnum mid ealle** (52 g) 'with weapons and all'. **brecan**, *briċþ*, *bræc*, *brǣcon*, *gebrocen* 'break'. **þæt firwit** 'curiosity' —*hine firwit bræc* 'he was curious'. **hwæt** 90 g. **wǣren** 90 g (mood).

118. **rīdan**, *rād*, *ridon* 66 g. **niþer** 'down'. **þæt spere** 33. **ā·cweċċan**=*cweċċan*, *cweahte* 'shake'. **unforht** 93 g. **ġewǣpnod** 'armed'. **þæt langsċip** 6 g. **werian**, *werede* 'defend'. **þȳ·lǣsþe** 20. **se sċiphere** 'fleet'. **nǣfre** 108 g. **openlīċe** 'openly'; **open** 'open'.

119. **miċel** here 'tall'. **sum** 'some one', here 'one'. **ġerīsan**, *-rās* 'befit'; compare *ġerisenlīċe* 90. **būtan** 52. **sēo ansien** 'countenance, what is seen, sight'; *ġesēon*. **lēogan** 98. **witan** 84 g. **hwanon** 92 g. **furþor** 115. **sċēawian**, *-ōde* 65 g. **se sǣmann** 108 g; observe the invidious suggestion of the idea 'pirate'. **ānfeald** 'plain', literally 'onefold'. **se ġeþoht** 'thought, intention'. **sēo ofost** 'speed, haste'. **cȳþan** 'make known'; *cūþ*.

120. **æþele** 'noble, excellent'. **hold** 'friendly, gracious, faithful'. **se hyġe** 'mind, heart'; compare *hyġelīest* 90. **þæt ǣrende** 93. **dieġle** 83. **unāsęcgendliċ** 'indescribable'; *ā·sęcgan* 'relate'. **yfel** plur. **mid·þǣmþe** 'with that that, by'. **for·swelgan** 20. **þiestre** 'dark'; compare *þīestro* 102. **se rǣd** 74. **lǣran** 74, here with acc. of the person. **ofer·swīþan** 'overcome'; *swīþ* 'strong', whence *swīþe* 'very'. **sēo bōt** 108. **onsǣġe** 100.

121. **ġedafenian** 51 g. **þæt ġesċēad** 'difference'. **iċ þæt ġehīere þæt** . . 'I hear (that, namely) that . . .' **þæt werod** 'troop'; *wer* 63. **ġewītan** 109. **wīsian**, *wīsode* 106 g, with dat. **swelċe ēac**=*ēac swelċe* 48. **bebēodan** 74 g, 75 g; *bēodan*, *bīett*, *bēad*, *budon*, *ġeboden* 'offer'. **beran** 9. **swelċ** 56. **ġifeþe** 'granted' adjective. **him ġesunde** (116) **beorgan** (110) 'preserve themselves so as to be uninjured', *ġesunde* agreeing with *hīe*.

122. **lǣtan** 106. **behindan** adv., prep. with dat. 'behind'. **se ancor** 'anchor'. **fæst** 16. **him** 104. **forþ** 'forth, forwards'. **hęreġeatwa** 115. **se helm** 'helmet'. **þæt hēafod** 1. **se eofor** 'wild boar'. **þæt līc** 103. **sēo anliċnes** 'likeness, image'; *anliċ* 'like'. **tō·þǣmþæt** 'in order that'. **fēorum** 47 g. **sēo frēċennes** 49.

123. **mǣre** 91. **se hrōf** 'roof'. **frætwian** 99. **þæt leoht** 99. **sċīnan** 1. **se ġiest** 'stranger, guest'. **tǣċan** 21. **hīe** (acc.) **ġeręstan** 'rest themselves'. **þæt mǣl** 85. **fēran** 111. **iċ tō sǣ wile** 'I am going to the sea'; verbs of motion are often omitted in this way. **se unfriþhęre** 'hostile army or fleet'; *friþ* 93. **sēo weard** 117.

124. **sēo stānstrǣt**=*strǣt* 34 g. **ā·lęcgan** 'lay down';

lęcgan, lęgþ, lęġde 'lay'. **se sċield** 'shield'. **se weall** 115. **sēo hyrne** 'corner'; *se horn* 'horn'. **æt·samne** 'together'; *samnian* 92. **sēo bęnċ** 'bench'. **wēriġ** 'weary'. **sēo faru** 'journey'; *faran* 47.

125. **hātte** 100. **se ǣrendraca** 93. **mōdiġ** 'proud'; *þæt mōd* 34. **sēo wēn** 'expectation, hope'—*wēn is* 'it is probable'; *wēnan* 108. **sēo mǣrþ** 'glory'; *mǣre* 91. **nealles** 48. **se wræcsīþ** 101—*for wræcsīþe* 'because of being exiled from your native land'.

126. **sēo gōdnes** 'goodness'. **unnan** infinitive of *ann, unnon, ūþe* 91 g. **mōt,** *þū mōst, mōton, mōste* 91 g.

127. **ā·bēodan** 'announce'; *bēodan* 121. **sēo andswaru** 32 g. **þǣr·rihte** 'immediately'. **cȳþan** 119.

128. **hrædlīċe** 74. **þǣr** 3. **se ealdormann** 57. **sēo eaxl** 'shoulder'. **þæt riht** 108. **feorran-cumen** 'come from afar, foreign', 25 g. **se lātteow** 'guide, leader'. **wiernan** 'deny, refuse'. **wierþe** 58. **þynċan** 4. **hwæt,** plur. *hwate* 'brisk, bold'. **se dōm** 'judgement, sentence, glory'. **belęcgan** 'cover, credit with' 124. **hūru** 'at any rate, however, certainly'. **dēah** 111. **lǣdan** 59.

129. **se cniht** 'boy'. **se nefa** 'grandson' 113. **hold** 120. **se frēond** 'friend', plur. *frīend*; compare *fēond* 92. **se sċipmann** 'sailor'. **sēo sęlen** 'gift'; compare *sęllan*. **sēo stręnġo** 'strength'; *strang*. **fultum** 91 g. **se brōga** 'terror'. **māþm** 98. **se snelsċipe** 'bravery'. **ofost** 119. **se wilcuma** 'wished-for or welcome guest', also weak adj.; *se willa* 'desire, pleasure'.

130. **ċierran** 'turn' trans. and intrans.—*ċierran eft* 'return'. **sēo ġebyrd** 'birth, lineage'; *beran*. **on·bīdan** 'await'; *bīdan, bād, bidon, ġebiden* 'wait, await, expect'. **sēo sprǣċ** 75. **sēo ġeęndung** 'end, result'.

131. **ā·rās** 80. **se hēap** 'troop'. **lǣfan** 'leave'. **bæftan**

91 g. **under** 35 g. **se hrōf** 123. **þæt hē ġestōd** 'so that'. **se heorþ** 'hearth'. **fæġerum** (78) **wordum** 52 g.

132. **hāl** 'uninjured, healthy'—*hāl wes þū!* 'hail!' **mǣrliċ**=*mǣre* 91. **dǣda** 45 (case). **sēo ġeogoþ** 'youth'. **īdel** 'useless, trivial, idle (talk)'. **siþþan** 'since, when'. **sie** 98 g (mood).

133. **lǣran** 74. **wīg** 111. **blōdiġ** 'blood-stained'; *þæt blōd* 103. **þǣr** 'where, when'. **se eoton** 101. **se gārsęcg** 'ocean'. **for·slōg and for·dyde** 92. **fīfe**: numerals which are otherwise uninflected take the inflections of *Dęne* when used absolutely, without a noun. **bindan**, *bint*, *band*, *bundon*, *ġebunden* 'bind'.

134. **sēo bēn** 'request, prayer'—*þǣre bēne* 43 g. **nū** 'now that'. **þæt werod** 121. **fǣlsian**, *fǣlsode* 'make safe or pleasant, purify'; *fǣle* 100. **sēo rēþnes** 'ferocity'; *rēþe* 103. **ręċċan** 65, here with gen. **for·hycgan** 'despise, disdain'; *hycgan* 'think', *se hyġe* 120; for the prefix compare *for·bēodan* 'forbid', *bēodan* 'command'. **iċ þæt for·hycge þæt** .. 121. **swā** 'as, on the understanding that'. **bliþe** 104, here with dat. **þæt wīg** 133. **bær** plur. *bare* (compare *hwate* 128) 'bare'. **iċ him wiþ-fō** 'grasp against, contend'; compare *hē him on-bestæl* 103. **fō, biþ** 106 g (tense). **stiþ** 89. **ġemōt** 51 g. **tō·gædre** 'together'—*tō·gædre fōn* 'come in conflict, engage hand to hand'.

135. **wēn is** 125. **se siġe** 91. **unforhtlīċe** 'fearlessly', 118. **ā·feallan**=*feallan* 9. **bebyriġan** 'bury'. **sorgian**, *sorgode* 'be grieved or anxious, trouble oneself'. **on·sęndan**= *sęndan* 93. **sēo byrne** 'corslet, coat of mail'. **sēo lāf** 'relic, hierloom'; *lǣfan* 131. **þæt ġeweorc** 70. **sēo wyrd** 'fate'; *ġeweorþan* 'happen', *weorþan* 'become'. **ā** 'ever, always.' **sċeal** 16.

136. **þæt ġefeoht** 'fight, battle'. **se fultum** 129. **sēo sorg**

'sorrow, anxiety, solicitude'. **sēo iermþ** 99. **sēo hęrġung** 104. **se folgoþ** 91. **wanian** 7; *is ġewanod* active 108 g.

137. full adv. 'full, very'. **oft** 'often'. **bēotian** 'promise, vow, boast, boast, threaten'; *bēot* 98. **dagian** 109. **sēo benċ** 124. **beġēotan** 'cover (with liquid)'; *ġēotan, ġēat, guton, goten* 'pour'. **þȳ** 36. **lǣs** 'less' adv. is used also like a noun, with the gen.

138. sīte 104. **blīþe** 134. **hwęttan,** *hwętte* 'sharpen, incite'; *hwæt* 128.

139. wistfullian, *-ode* 'feast'; *sēo wist* 'food, feast, luxury'. **rȳman** 'make room, clear'; *þæt rūm* 'space'. **æt·samne** 124. **behealdan** 'practise, watch'; *healdan* 62. **se byrele** 'cup-bearer, butler'; *beran*. **sēo notu** 'employment, office'; cp. *sēo nytt* 61, *notian* 72. **æfter** here 'along'. **se medo** 'mead'. **sċenċan** 'pour out'. **hlūtor** 'clear'. **þæt ealo** 86—*hlūtor ealo* was a superior kind of ale. **ġieddian** 10. **beorht** 'bright, clear'. **sēo stemn** 'voice'. **sēo ġesamnung** 'gathering'; *samnian*.

140. se fōt 18 g. **se þyle** 'orator'. **se Unferþ** 91. **æfestiġ** 'envious'. **ne unnan** 126 'grudge'. **sēo weorþmynt** 'glory, honour'; compare *weorþ* 60, *sēo ġemynd* 'memory, mind'. **se æfþanca** 'disgust, cause of displeasure'.

141. þæt sund 'swimming'. **flītan,** *flāt, fliton* 'contend, dispute'; *þæt ġeflit* 74. **ġit** 58 g. **þæt ġielp** 97 g. **þæt feorh** 122. **nēþan** 'risk, venture'. **se gārsęcg** 133. **lāþ** 'hostile'—*ne lēof ne lāþ* 'neither friend nor foe'. **for·wiernan**=*wiernan* 128. **seofon** 80. **niht** plur. of *sēo niht*—*seofon niht* 'seven days'; compare the similar use of the plur. *winter* 107. **sēo ȳþ** 'wave'. **swincan** 16. **ofer·flītan** 'overcome in a contest'. **eard** 110. **sēo stręnġo** 129. **weorpan** 39. **befullan** 'fully'. **ġelǣstan** 93. **wiersa** comparative of *yfel* 'bad'. **sēo ġemēting** 'meeting'—*ġemētinge* gen. **bīdan** 130. **sēo nēawist** 'proximity'; *nēah* 7 g, *wesan* 102 g.

142. **hwæt** 'lo!' **īdel** 132—*fela īdles* 'much of what is idle, much nonsense'. **þæt sōþ** 49—*tō sōþe* 'in truth'. **unc Brecan** (both acc.) 'me and Breca'. **ġelimpan** 91.

143. **se cnihthād** 'boyhood'; *cniht* 129. **ġecweþan** 'agree'. **ġebēotian** 137. **nacod** 'bare'. **þohton** 78. **þæt dēor** 'wild beast'; cp. *wildēor* 26. **węrian** 118. **oþ·swimman** 'swim away from' w. dat., 12.

144. **yfele** 'badly'; *yfel* 'bad', *þæt yfel* 'evil' 103. **sēo faru** 124. **þæt unc on-becōm** . . 'namely that . .' **hrēoh** 'rough, severe'. **þæt weder** 'weather'. **wōd** 'mad, raging'. **strang** 105. **se norþwind** 'north wind'. **wīde** 'widely, far'; *wīd* 'wide'. **tō·drīfan** 'drive apart'.

145. **ā·hwęttan**=*hwęttan* 138. **se grund** 'bottom, depths'. **tēon** 116. **hwæþre**=*þēah·hwæþre* 65. **se Dryhten** 'the Lord'. **for·ġiefan** 'grant, give'; *ġiefan, ġeaf, ġēafon, ġiefen* 'give'. **of·stingan** 'stab to death'; *stingan, stang, stungon* 'pierce'. **þæt wundor** 109. **āna** 109. **ā·węrian**=*węrian*. **þæt lēan** 'reward, requital'. **for·ġieldan** 108. **ehtan** 42 g. **næfde**=*ne hæfde*. **se ġefēa** 46 g. **him tō męte** 'as their food'. **þicgan,** *þiġede* 'take, eat.' **licgan** 99. **uppe** 10, 'on the surface.' **for·wundian,** *-ode* 'wound severely'. **nigon** 'nine'. **se nicor** 'water-monster'.

146. **sūþan** 'from the south'. **ġestillan** 'calm'; **stille** 'quiet.' **tō þǣm þæt** 'to such a degree that'. **wēriġ** 124. **furþor** 119.

147. **se bana** 'murderer, cause of death'. **sēo hęll** 'hell'. **þæt wīte** 'punishment, torment'. **drēogan** 108. **þæt ġewitt** 'understanding.' **duge** 111. **tęllan** 3. **on·findan** 'find out, perceive'; *findan* 114. **sēo fǣhþ** 106. **on·drǣdan,** *on·drēd* 'fear'. **tō Dęnum** 'at the hands of, from'. **se wīgcræft**

'strategy, warfare'. **tō·morgen** 'to-morrow' compare *tō·dæġ* 30. **ġehwelċ** 83. **orsorg** 'without anxiety, secure'; *sorg* 136.

148. **ġelīefan** 'believe'. **sēo help** 111. **fæstrǣd** 'firm, stedfast'; *se rǣd* 74. **se ġeþoht** 119.

149. **sēo cwēn** 32 g. **ǣrest** adv. 'first'. **sēo cuppe** 'cup'.

150. **ġeong** 'young'. **snotor** 'sagacious, wise'. **se willa** 129. **sēo frōfor** 'consolation'. **lange** 63.

151. **on·fōn** 5 with acc. or gen. **on·bryrdan** 'inspire, excite'. **āhwæþer** 'either'. **lēode** plur. 'people'. **tō·niht** 'to-night'. **se þeġnsċipe** 'manliness, bravery'; *se þeġn*. **cȳþan** 119. **se ęnde** 'end'.

153. **sēo bliss** 99. **se hleahtor** 'laughter'. **betǣċan** 21. **þæt ġemōtærn** 'meeting-house'; *ġemōt* 134, *ærn* 62. **æþele** 120. **ġemyne** imper. of *ġeman, þū ġemanst, ġemunon, ġemunde* 'remember'. **wacian** 21. **þæt gōd** 79. **se wana** 'want, lack'; *wanian* 136.

154. **feohtan,** *feaht* 'fight'. **lǣfan** 131. **ān** has plur. *āne* 'only, alone'.

155. **sēo byrne** 135. **of** 33 g. **se helm** 122. **se hand-þeġn** 'attendant'. **samod** 'together, also'. **earg** 'cowardly'. **ēaþe** 58. **cann** 'knows (how to), can'. **wealdan,** *wēold* 'control, wield'. **ofer·sittan** 'abstain from'. **dēman** 'judge, decide'. **swā hwæþer swā** 'whichever'. **þæt ġemet** 92.

156. **on·hieldan** 'bend, lay down'. **þæt bolster** 'bolster'. **swā same** 'likewise'. **frīend** 126. **slǣp** 32 g. **on·ġēan** 33, here prep. w. acc. **se cyme** 'coming'. **ierre** 'angry'.

157. **ā·wierġed** 6 g. **stealcian,** *-ode* 'stalk'. **þiċċe** 'thick'. **se mist** 'mist'. **besierwan,** *-sierede* 'circumvent, take by surprise'; cp. *ġierwan, ġierede,* 114.

158. **arn** 1. **sēo duru** 19 g. **on·ġietan** 'understand, perceive', inflected like *beġietan* 38. **fæste** adverb of *fæst* 122. **belūcan,** *-lēac, -lucon, -locen* 'lock, close'. **læhte** 26.

swīþliċ=*swīþ* 120. **sēo miht** 'strength, power'. **se heorr** 'hinge'. **ā·hōf** 104. **stōd** 'stood, shone'. **þæt fȳr** 11.

159. **ā·hliehhan**=*hliehhan*, *hlōg* 'laugh'. **behēold** 139. **faran** 47, 'act'.

160. **ieldan** 'delay'; *eald.* **styċċemǣlum** 5 g. **tō·breġdan** 'tear to pieces'; *breġdan* 33 g. **tō·brecan** 'break to pieces'; *brecan* 117. **þæt bān** 'bone'. **se tusċ** 'tusk'. **sēo ǣdre** 'vein'. **se līchama** 103. **mid ealle** 117.

161. **licgende** for *licgendne*; *licgan* 145. **ġesittan** 'sit up'. **se earm** 'arm'—*ġesæt wiþ earm* 'leaned on his elbow'. **on·ġeat** 158. **ġemētan** 'meet with, find, experience'.

162. **forht** 34. **flēon**, *flīehþ*, *flēah* 'flee'. **sēo wunung** 'dwelling'. **se sċucca** 6 g. **se drohtoþ** 'way of life, condition, circumstances'; *drohtian* 84. **swelċe** 'as'.

163. **ġemunde** 153. **ūplang** 'upright'. **fæstlīċe** 33. **ūtweard** 'outwards, towards the door'. **fæstor** compar. of the adverb *fæste* 158. **ful·nēah** 'very nearly,' 137. **berstan** 49. **unġemetliċ** 92, 52 g. **se nīþ** 'violence, hostility'. **winnan** 101. **dynian**, *dynede* 'resound'. **sēo syll** 'foundation, setting'. **ā·būgan** 'be bent or pulled'; *būgan* 90. **ā·hrēosan** = *hrēosan*, *hrēas*, *hruron*, *ġehroren* 75 g. **grundlunga** 'from the foundations, completely'; *grund* 144. **sēo īsenbęnd** 'iron bond, clamp'. **besmiþian** 'cover, fit (with metal)'. **innan** 'inside'. **for·bærnan** 'burn' trans.

164. **bēġen** 'both' is inflected like *twēġen* 56 g. **ymb·þrinġan**, *-þrang*, *-þrungon* 'crowd round, surround'. **hēawan**, *hēow* 'hew, cut'. **nyste** 109 g. **for·swęrian** 'forswear, renounce, be proof against'; *swęrian* 94. **se drȳcræft** 'sorcery'; *se drȳ* 'magician' (originally 'druid').

165. **hrīeman** 'shout, yell'; *hrēam* 17. **ęġeslīċe** adv. from *ęġesliċ* 'terrible'; *se ęġesa* 'terror, fear' (compare *se ęġe*). **furþum** 62. **se weard** 117. **ā·fyrht** 'terrified'.

166. sēo wund 108 g. **ġesīene** 105. **sēo eaxl** 128. **sēo sinu** 'sinew'. **on·springan** 'crack'; *springan, sprang, sprungon* 'spring'. **tō·berstan**=*berstan*. **se dēaþ** 32 g. **wundian** 'wound'. **flēah** 162. **ġefrēdan** 'feel'. **þēah** 'however'.

167. þæt ġielp 141. **fǣlsian** 134. **bētan** 'mend, cure'; *sēo bōt* 120. **sweotol** 105. **þæt tācen** 'sign, proof'. **se stapol** 'flight of steps'. **dura** dat. of *sēo duru* 158. **sēo wǣfersien** 'spectacle'; compare *sēo ansīen* 119.

168. sēo męniġo 19 g. **nēan** 'from near'; *nēah* 'near' adj. and adv. **se dēaþ** 166. **sārliċ** 'grievous'; *þæt sār* 'pain, grief'.

169. se męre 35 g. **se nicor** 145. **drēfan** 'make turbid or sad'.

170. him 122. **hāmweard** 'homewards'. **se hagosteald-mann** 'bachelor'.

171. se weġ 27 g. **norþ** adv. 'in the north, north'. **sūþ** adv. 'in the south, south'. **wierþe** 128. **tǣlan** 'blame'. **hūru** 128.

172. ærnan 'gallop', literally 'make to run', from *iernan* —*on ġeflit* (74) *ærnan* 'race'. **fæġer** 'fair, good'.

173. sēo lēoþwise 'metre'; *lēoþ* 112, *wīse* 50. **ā·sęcgan** 120. **wel-ġesętt** 'well composed'. **se wręċċa** 'exile, knight errant'; *wracu* 101. **bēġen** 164. **se ēam** 'uncle'. **him āna** 'alone by himself'; the *him* is pleonastic.

174. se draca 'dragon'. **þæt scræf** 'cave'. **ā·cwęllan,** *-cwealde* 'kill'. **hār** 'hoary, grey'. **nēþan** 141. **hętelīċe** 'violently'; *se hęte* 'hatred, violence'. **þiede** 17. **æt·standan** 'stand still'. **meltan,** *mealt* 'melt' intrans. **sēo hǣte** 38 g. **for·swǣlan** 'burn up'. **snelsċipe** 129. **þæt goldhord** 'treasure (of gold)'. **ġegān** 'gain', literally 'get by going'.

176. mōdiġlīċe 'proudly', 125. **stæppan,** *stōp* 'step'. **on·middan** 100. **se hēap** 131. **samod** 155. **þæt mæġden** 'maiden'. **se stapol** 167.

177. se Dryhten 145. **se þanc** 'thanks'. **sēo ansien** 119. **þæt bismer** 'insult, humiliation'. **ġebīdan** 'await, endure'; *bīdan* 141. **ġēara** 'long ago'. **lēode** 151. **se sċucca** 162. **bewęrian** = *węrian* 118. **ā** 135. **feorrancund** 'foreign, from afar'; compare *godcund* 90. **þurh·tēon** 'accomplish'; *tēon*. **ūre** gen. **sēo snytro** 'wisdom'; *snotor* 150. **hwæt** 142. **ġeberan** 'bear, bring forth'. **ġiet** 79. **leofaþ** 11. **ēstiġ** 'gracious'. **se bearntēam** 'child-bearing'.

178. lēofa 68. **nū** 'now that 134, since (causal)'. **lufian**, *lufode* 'love'. **forþ** 'forwards 122, in future'. **nīwe** 51 g. **sēo sibb** 74. **se wana** 153. **þæs-þe** 63 g. **þæt ġeweald** 'power, control'; *wealdan* 155. **lēanian**, *-ode* 'reward, requite' with dat. of the person and acc. of the thing; *þæt lēan* 145. **wāc** 'weak, insignificant'. **se dōm** 128.

179. þæt ġeswinc 56. **þæt ġewinn** 'warfare'. **blīþeliċe** adv. from *blīþe* 138. **mōste** 126. **ūþe** 126. **se flēam** 'flight'. **for·wiernan** 141. **æt·fēolan** 'adhere, stick to'; *fēolan, fealh, fulgon* 'enter'. **þæt fēþe** 'movement, walking'. **for·lǣtan** 74. **þēah** 166. **se earm** 161. **behindan** 122. **lęngra** compar. of *lang* 55 g. **dēop** 75. **se dōm** 128. **on·bīdan** 130. **dēman** 155.

180. ġeswīgian 'be silent' with gen. **se finger** 2 g. **se næġel** 'nail'. **heard** 3 g. **þæt stīele** 'steel'. **sċearp** 'sharp'. **for·ċeorfan** 'cut off'; *ċeorfan, ċearf* 33 g.

181. innan 163. **wer** 63. **ġearcian** 61. **se wāg** 'wall'. **dēorwierþe** 58. **þæt godewębb** 'precious cloth, purple'. **bewrēon**, *-wrāh, -wrigon* 'cover'.

182. tō·brecan 160. **innanweard** 'inside'. **ofer eall** (neut.) 'everywhere'. **se heorr** 158. **tō hlīdan**, *-hlād, -hlidon, -hliden* 'be broken open, split'. **þurh·wunian** 100. **ansund** 'sound, entire'; *ġesund* 116.

183. blissian, *-ode* 'rejoice in' with gen., 'be festive'; *sēo* *bliss* 99. **bet** adv. of *betera*; compare *leng* 107, *lengra* 179. **ġebǣran** 90.

184. for·ġiefan 145. **gylden** 'of gold'. **se seġn** 'banner'. **þæt lēan** 108. **þorfte** 108. **sċamian** 'be ashamed'. **sēo ġiefu** 'gift'. **eahta** 'eight'. **se sadol** 'saddle'. **þæt wīghors** 'war-horse'. **brūcan** 62. **manlīċe** 'like a man'. **lēanian** 178. **se þeġnsċipe** 151.

185. þā·ġiet=*ġiet* 'yet, in addition'. **þone ānne** 48. **mid fēo for·ġieldan** 108. **ā·cwealde** 174.

186. þæt lēoþ 112. **sēo burg** 18 g, dat. *byriġ*; compare *þǣre sylh* 16.

187. ā·singan 'sing to an end'. **se hleahtor** 153. **þæt gamen** 'sport, merriment'. **þæt wīn** 59. **þæt fæt** 72.

188. sēo cynewiþþe 'diadem'; *cyne-stōl* 96, *sēo wiþþe* 'withy, chaplet'. **se ēam** 173.

189. þæt cyneriċe 'kingdom'. **glæd** 'cheerful, kind'. **ġemǣne** 'common'. **ārlīċe** 'kindly'; *sēo ār* 'honour, mercy, kindness'. **se willa** 150.

190. se æþeling 'young noble, heir apparent'; **æþele** 120. **þæt hræġl** 'dress, robe'. **iewan** 'show'. **se healsbēag** 'torque'; *se heals* 'neck', *bēag* 36.

191. ġeþēoh imper. of *ġeþēon*, *ġeþāh* 'prosper'. **līþe** 'gentle, kind'. **se lārēow** 89. **iċ þē þæs lēan ġeman** 'I will bear in mind a reward to thee for that'. **þæt lof** 80. **ā·rǣran** 'raise'; *a·rīsan*. **ǣghwelċ** 'each'. **ġetrīewe** 20. **ġeþwǣre** 74. **lustlīċe** 53.

193. ġeęndian 130.

194. mēder dat. of *sēo mōdor* 11 g. **se būr** 107.

195. þæt bedd 80. **þæt bolster** 156. **ġeond·brǣdan** 'cover or spread throughout'; *brǣdan* 'make broad, spread', from *brād* 4. **ġehęnde** 'near'. **se þēaw** 103. **ealneweġ** 27 g. **æt hām** 16. **ūte** 60. **þæt folc** 57.

196. **on·slǣpan** 'fall asleep'. **on·ġieldan** 'pay for'; *ġieldan* 93. **sārlīċe** adv. of *sārlīċ* 168. **sēo nihtrest** 'night rest'. **se nīþ** 163. **se wrecend** 66 g 'avenger'. **ilca** 60. **se ġefēa** 145. **sēo ġedrēfednes** 'sadness', 169. **ċierran** 130. **fealh** 179. **næs** 79.

197. **ā·hafen** 104. **se brōga** 129. **ā·fyrht** 165. **on·funden** 147. **teohhian**, *-ode*, 'appoint'. **hangian**, *-ode* 35 g.

198. **dēad** 'dead'. **fetian** 'fetch'. **bīdan** 141. **āsċian** 76. **ġetǣse** 'pleasant, comfortable'. **wǣre** 'had been'.

199. **þā ġesǣlþa** 63 g. **nīwian**, *-ode* 'renew'; *nīwe* 51 g. **ieldra** 55 g. **þæt ġefeoht** 136. **se fēþa** 'band of infantry, troop'; compare *fēþe* 179. **hnītan** 7 g, *hnāt*, *hniton*. **cnyssan**, *cnysede* 'clash'.

200. **se bana** 147. **oþ·flēon** 'escape'; *flēon* 162. **wrecan** *wræc*, *wrǣcon* 'avenge'. **þe** 2. **ġiestran-niht** 'yesterday night'; compare *ġiestran-dæġ* 30. **ā·feallan** 135.

201. **ūplendisċ mann** 'rustic, up-country man'. **swelċe** plur. of *swelċ*. **hwearfian**, *-ode* 'wander'; compare *ġeond·hweorfan* 99. **ōþer . . ōþer** 'one . . the other'. **þæs-þe** 4. **anlīċ** 122. **se wæstm** 'growth, stature, form'. **nemnan** 'name'; *se nama*. **ealddagas** 'days of yore'. **hwæþer** 53.

202. **eardian**, *-ode* 'dwell'; *se eard*. **wēste** 'desert'; compare *þæt wēsten* 101. **ǣmenne** 'solitary', literally 'without men'. **nabbaþ**=*ne habbaþ*. **se wulf** 20. **þæt wildēor** 26. **ġefēre** 'accessible'; *fēran* 123. **sċearp** 180, here 'rugged'. **stāniht** 'stony'. **hēah** 3 g has plur. *hēa*, dat. *hēam* with contraction 46 g. **þæt clif** 115. **wilde** 109. **sēo ēa** 39. **unġefōglīċ** 'impetuous'. **se strēam** 'current, stream'. **sċēotan** 43. **se gārsecg** 133.

203. **heonon** 'hence'. **hār** 174. **ā·weaxan** 'grow out'; *weaxan* 7. **hrīmiġ** 'rimy'; *se hrīm* 'rime, hoar-frost'. **bearwas** plur. of *se bearo* 'grove, wood'. **ofer·helmian**, *-ode* 'overhang'; *se helm*. **neoþan** 'below'; compare *niþer* 118. **biernan,** *barn* 'burn' intrans.

204. se ęġesa 165. **sēo ānnes** 'solitude'. **wīdġille** 'extensive'. **nǣniġ** 'not any, no'. **ā·drēogan** 63 **beflēon** 'avoid'; *flēon* 162. **se heorot** 29. **se wudu** 54. **se ōfer** 'bank'. **for·lǣtan** 179. **unhīere** 'cheerless, dismal'. **hrēoh** 144. **riġnan** 'rain'; *se reġn* 9. **wēope** 104.

205. rǣd 74. **ān** here 'alone'. **ġelang** 'attainable'. **frēċne** 49. **dyrre** 16. **on·weġ** 'away', lit. 'on the road'.

206. snotra 150, 68 (inflection). **bętere** 53 g. **murnan** 106. **ǣġhwelċ** 192. **ġebīdan** 177. **æfter his dæġe** 34 g. **uton** 74. **ġehātan** 'promise'. **losian** 58. **þȳs dæġe** 'this day'; *þȳs* instrumental of *þes* (compare *þȳ* 36). **sēo ġeþyld** 'patience'; *þolian* 102. **tō** here 'from'.

207. ā·hlēapan 'leap up'; *hlēapan, hlēop* 'leap'. **se lāst** 'track'. **īeþġesīene** 'easy to see'; *īeþe* 'easy' (*ēaþe* 'easily' 155), *ġesīene* 105. **drīfan** (16) **þæt spor** (105) 'follow up the track'. **se æcer** 16. **sēo mǣd,** plur. *mǣdwa* 'meadow'. **bȳne** adj. 'inhabited'; *būn* 100. **se weald** 'forest'.

208. se pæþ 'path', plur. *paþas*. **sticol** 'steep, rough'. **nearo** 'narrow', plur. *nearwe*; cp. *ġearo* 26. **fēowera** gen. of *fēower* 3 g used absolutely 133—*fēowera sum* (119) 'one of four', that is 'with three others'. **fǣringa**=*fǣrlīċe* 33. **for·sēarian,** *-ode* 'wither'. **se bēam** 35 g. **hangian** 197. **under·neoþan**=*neoþan* 203.

209. wearþ him ange on mōde 'he was anxious or distressed in mind'; *ange* is the adverb of *ęnġe* 'narrow, distressing'. **ġemētan** 161. **blāwan** 71. **se horn** 124. **wīsian** 71. **sēo nǣdre** 'serpent'. **se draca** 174. **se næss** 'headland, promontory'. **hrēosan** 163 'fall, rush'. **sēo flān** 'arrow'. **of·scēotan** 'shoot to death'; *scēotan* 202; compare *of·stingan* 145, *of·slēan*. **lęttan** 'hinder'. **þæt sund** 141.

tō·stician 'stab severely'; compare *of·stician* 32. **se hōc** 'hook'. **sċēawian** 119. **ęġeslić** 165. **se ġiest** 123.

210. ġierede 114. **cræftiġ** 'skilful'. **besęttan** 'set round (with), cover'. **bītan,** *bāt, biton* 'bite, cut'. **ǣnlić** 'unique, excellent'; *ān*. **on·lāh** strong preterite of the weak *on·lǣnan* 'lend'. **se þyle** 140. **sēo þearf** 114. **sēo lāf** 135. **swīcan,** *swāc, swicon* 'fail'; compare *beswīcan* 50. **hūru** 128. **ǣrra** comparative adj. corresponding to the adv. *ǣr* 'former'. **hrēom** dat. of *hrēoh* 204. **ā·licgan** 'fail, perish'. **þā** (then) **æt nīehstan** 'thereupon, then'; *nīehst* superl. of *nēah* 168. **bemetan** 'estimate'; *metan, mæt* 'measure'. **naht,** *nāwiht* neut. 'nothing'—*hine tō nahte bemetan* 'think himself of no account'.

211. ġeþęnċan 'consider'. **fūs** 89 g. **sīþian** 'set out'; *sīþ* 91. **ġesprecan** 'discuss, agree on'. **þæt stǣl** 'place, stead'. **se forþsīþ** 'departure, death'. **se mundbora** 'protector, patron'. **on·sęndan** 135. **on·ġietan** 158. **starian** 'gaze'. **cystiġ** 51 g. **mīn dēorwierþe sweord** is the one mentioned in 184. **Hrunting** is the name of Unferþ's sword.

212. efstan 'hasten'; *ofost* 119. **sċēat** 202. **dūfan,** *dēaf, dufon* 'dive'. **þæt spell** 68.

213. under þǣm 'meanwhile'. **on·findan** 147. **ufan** 'from above'. **fandian,** *-ode* 'test, explore'; *findan*. **grīpan,** *grāp, gripon* 'grasp'. **tō·ġēanes** prep. with dat. 'towards, to meet'. **sēo clāwu** 'claw'. **naht lāþes** 'nothing hostile, no injury' 210, 141. **īsen** 71. **se hring** 'ring (of the corslet)'. **þurh·fōn** 'penetrate'. **befōn** 'encompass, clasp'. **wealdan** 155. **swęnċan** 'afflict, persecute'; *swincan* 141. **tusċ** 160.

214. se flōd 'flood, water'; *flōwan, flēow* 'flow'. **dęrian,** *dęrede* 'injure'. **inne on** 'in'. **beorhte** adv. of *beorht* 7 g.

215. mihtiġ 'mighty'. **rǣsan** 9 g. **slōg** 107 g. **hlēoþrian,** *-ode* 'resound'. **se dynt** 'stroke'. **se forma sīþ** 'the first time'. **ā·læġ** 210.

216. **ānrǣd** 'resolute'; cp. *ānmōd* 90, *fæstrǣd* 148. **of·dūne** 9. **ġetrīewan** 'trust'. **langsum** 'lasting'; compare *ġehiersum* 90. **þæt word** here 'reputation'. **carian**, *-ode* 'care'. **rohte** 134. **þæt feax** 'head of hair'. **grimme** adv. of *grimm* 'fierce, cruel'. **for·ġeald** 145. **ofer·weorpan** 'throw backwards, on the back'. **se fiell** 'fall'—*on fielle weorþan* 'fall'. **þæt seax** 'short sword'.

217. **hæfde** subj. **for·sīþian** 'perish', literally 'make a disastrous expedition'; *sīþian* 211. **ġesċildan** 'protect'; *se sċield*. **ā·standan** 'stand up'; compare *ā·hlēapan* 207. **se wāg** 181. **orwēna** adj. 'despairing'; *sēo wēn* 125; compare *orsorg* 147. **sēo sċēaþ** 'sheath'. **ā·tēah** 9. **hętelīċe** 174. **se heals** 190. **þurh·wadan** 'penetrate'; *wadan*, *wōd* 'wade, go'. **þæt flǣsċ** 62. **bānhringas** 'vertebræ'; *bān* 160, *hring* 213. **ā·sīgan**=*sīgan*, *sāg*, *sigon* 'sink, fall, descend, go'; compare *onsǣġe* 100. **ā·lǣtan** 'let go, send forth, give up'.

218. **ġefeah** 94. **miċlum ġefēan**: here *miċlum* is equivalent to *miċle* 52 g. **wilnian**, *-ode* 'desire'. **unā·rīmedlīċ** 'innumerable'; *ā·rīman* 'count up', *þæt rīm* 'number'. **þæt bodiġ** 'trunk, body'. **wīde** 144. **sprang** 166. **windan**, *wand*, *wundon* 'wind, roll'. **sēo flōr** 'floor'.

219. **wēndon** 108, 89 g (mood). **untwēogendlīċe** 'without doubt'; *twēogan* or *twēon*, *twēode* 'doubt', *se twēo* acc. *twēon* (46 g) 'doubt'.

220. **þæt nōn** 80. **forlēton** 74. **belīfan** *-lāf*, *-lifon*, 'remain'; *sēo lāf* 135. **se ōfer** 204. **sēoc** 'ill'. **starian** 211. **wȳsċan** 'wish'.

221. **under þǣm** 213. **se ęnt** 'giant'. **wanian** 7. **se īses ġiecel** 'icicle'; *þæt īs* 'ice'. **tō þǣm** 'to that degree'. **hāt** 'hot'. **ǣtren** 'poisonous'; *þæt ātor* 'poison'. **ġemealt** 174. **þæt hilt** 'hilt'. **ān** 205. **ęlles** 107.

222. **wearþ on sunde** 'began to swim'; compare *wearþ on fielle* 216. **dēaf** 212.

223. **sēo byrþen**, gen. *byrþenne* 'burden'. **of dydon** 155. **drēopan**, *drēap* 'drip'. **męnġan** 6 g.

224. **earfoþliċe** adv. of *earfoþ* 'difficult'. **se stęnġ** 'pole'. **þæt feax** 216. **mōdor** gen. **wǣfersien** 167. **wundrian**, *-ode* 'wonder' with gen. **seldcūþ** 59. **sēo ġesihþ** 4.

225. **þæt lāc** 'gift, offering'. **þæt tācen** 167. **ġeēode** 174. **for·weorþan** 'perish'; compare *for·sīþian* 217.

226. **ġeweorþan** 'happen'—*hū hine hæfde geworden* 'how he had fared'. **ġehātan** 206. **se hearm** 'injury, insult'. **on·drǣdan** 147. **sēo healf** 2.

227. **ā·ġiefan**=*ġiefan*. **fæġere** adv. of *fæġer*. **mearcian**, *-ode* 'mark'. **ā·tiefran** 'paint, draw'. **flōd** 214. **ǣrest** adj., adv. 149. **rūnstafas** 'runic letters'. **hwǣm** 'for whom'.

228. **swīgian** 180. **lā** 16. **eall þæs þe** 'all (of) that which'. **þæt lof** 191. **ūpāhafen** 'lifted up, elated, arrogant'. **sēo ġeþyld** 206; abstract nouns are often used in the plur. with singular meaning. **hieltst** 62.

229. **ġeweaxan** 'grow up'; *weaxan* 91. **sēo forwyrd** 'destruction'; *for·weorþan* 225. **ā·mierran** 'destroy'. **ā·flieman** 'expel'; *se flēam* 179. **hwearflan** 201. **ġegōdian**, *-ode* 'endow'; *gōd*. **grōwan**, *grēow* 'grow'. **hwæþre** 145. **sēo wælhrēownes** 'cruelty'. **sēo ġītsung** 'avarice'. **sēo uncyst** 'vice'; compare *cystiġ* 211. **þæt bīspell** 'example'; *spell* 212. **ā·ręċċan**, *ā·reahte* 'relate'; compare *ǣrendraca* 93.

230. **sēo ġiefu** 184. **męnn** dat. of *se mann*; compare dat. *byriġ* 186—*þǣm męnn* 'to a man': 'the' is often used to show that the noun is to be taken in an abstract sense. **him his willan tō-forlǣtt** 'grants him what he wishes'. **sēo wynn** 'joy'. **under·þiedd** 96. **se unwīsdōm** 'folly'. **wista** 139 'luxury'; compare *ġeþylda* 228. **swęnċan** 213.

sēo ādl 'disease'. **drę̇ċċan,** *dręċþ, dreahte* 'afflict'. **se unfriþhęre** 123.

231. þæt wierse 141 'the less pleasant side of things, adversity'. **on·innan** prep. with dat. 'within'. **ofermētto** plur. 19 g, 228 'pride'; *ofermōd* 'proud'. **se ęnġel** 'angel'. **sēo sāwol** 'soul'. **ġieman** 'regard, take care of' with gen. **se boga** 'bow'. **fācenliċe** 'treacherously'; *þæt fācen* 78. **sēo heorte** 63. **of·sċoten** 209. **biter** 'bitter, painful'. **sēo flān** 209. **him on hand gǣþ** 'surrenders to him'. **þæt bebod** 'command'; *bebēodan* 121.

232. se wela 57. **þæt unġemet** 92. **se ġītsere** 'miser'; *sēo ġītsung* 229. **hordian,** *-ode* 'hoard'; *þæt hord* 174. **hwīlwęndliċ**=*hwīlwęnde* 'temporary'; *sēo hwīl.* **sēo spēd,** *þā spēda* 'riches'; *spēdiġ* 87. **for·ġietan,** *-ġeat* 70 g. **for·ġieman** 'neglect'; *ġieman* 231. **tōweard** 'future'.

233. fǣġe 'fated to die'. **fēhþ tō** 92. **unhnēawliċe** 'ungrudgingly'. **ne ġiemþ nā his ęġes** 'does not care for the fear of him'='does not fear his anger'.

234. for·būgan 'avoid'; *būgan* 36. **ēċe rǣd** (74) 'eternal good'. **sēo ġeogoþ** 132. **se blǣd** 'prosperity, prime'. **beniman** 'deprive'; *niman.* **se fęnġ** 'grasp'; *fōn.* **se wielm** 'boiling, surging'. **se bearhtm** 'glance' (*beorht*)—*ēagena bearhtm* 'the evil eye'. **for·flēon** 'escape'; *flēon* 162.

235. heardliċe 'vigorously, bravely'. **bewęrian** 177. **se wiþerwinna** 'adversary'; *wiþer-* 'against', *winnan* 101. **sēo edwęnden** 'change, reverse'. **unlibbende** 'dead'. **þæt setl** 109.

236. blissian 183. **miċlum** 'greatly'. **wistfullian** 139. **sēo ġereordung** 'entertainment, feasting'.

237. se lust 53. **mēþiġ** 'tired'. **se sęleþeġn** 'chamberlain'. **ġeteohhian** 197. **þæt dæġred** 16. **bodian,** *-ode* 'announce'.

239. sēo lǣn 'loan'. **se þanc** 177. **hęrian,** *-ede* 'praise'. **leahtrian,** *-ode* 'blame'.

240. þæt cynesetl 109. **se cuma** 'stranger'. **fūs** 211. **bewęnian** 'treat (kindly)'; *węnian, -ede* 'accustom, wean'. **ūs wel dohtest** 'stoodest us in good stead'. **sēo nēahþēod** 'neighbouring nation'. **þūsend** 57 g. **se æþeling** 190. **tō Ġēata lande þęnċþ:** compare *iċ tō sǣ wile* 123. **fierlen** 'distant'; *feorr.*

241. þē dat. **snotorlīċe** adv. of *snotor.* **ęlles-hwæt** 'anything else', 107. **ġesǣlan** 'happen'; *ġesǣlþ* 63 g. **lifes bēon** 'be alive'. **bęt** 183—*swā lęnġ swā bęt* 'the longer the more'. **ġemǣne** 189. **fæstnian** 93. **ealles** 48. **fæstmōd** 'firm, constant, reliable'.

242. cyssan 'kiss'. **se heals** 217. **se tēar** 'tear'. **for·beran** 'restrain'. **se langoþ** 'longing'. **on·ǣlan** 'inflame'. **wȳsċan** 220. **wilnian** 218. **twēon** 219, here impersonal w. acc. of the pers. and gen. of the thing.

243. weorþian 74. **sēo cystiġnes** 'liberality, generosity'. **orleahtre** 'blameless'; compare *leahtrian* 239, *orwēna* 217. **benam** 234.

244. se hearm 226. **frēondlīċe** 'in a friendly manner'. **se ancor** 122. **hladan,** *hlōd, ġehladen* 'load'. **missenliċ** 34. **se bāt** 39. **golde-fǣted** 'ornamented with gold'. **wierþe** 58.

245. ġefæġen 94.

246. befriġnan 'question'. **sweotollīċe** adv. = *sweotole* 105. **sume þā māþmas:** *māþmas* in apposition to *sume.*

247. sēo landār 'estate'; *sēo ār* 189 has also the meaning 'revenue, property'. **sēo weorþung** 'honour, dignity'.

THE END.